Western political theory
in the face of the future

Themes in the
Social Sciences

Editors: Jack Goody & Geoffrey Hawthorn

The aim of this series is to publish books which will focus on topics of general and interdisciplinary interest in the social sciences. They will be concerned with non-European cultures and with developing countries, as well as with industrial societies. The emphasis will be on comparative sociology and, initially, on sociological, anthropological and demographic topics. These books are intended for undergraduate teaching, but not as basic introductions to the subjects they cover. Authors have been asked to write on central aspects of current interest which have a wide appeal to teachers and research students, as well as to undergraduates.

First books in the series

Edmund Leach: *Culture and Communication: the logic by which symbols are connected. An introduction to the use of structuralist analysis in social anthropology*

Anthony Heath: *Rational Choice and Social Exchange: A critique of exchange theory*

P. Abrams and A. McCulloch: *Communes, Sociology and Society*

Jack Goody: *The Domestication of the Savage Mind*

Jean-Louis Flandrin: *Families in Former Times: Kinship, household and sexuality*

Western political theory in the face of the future

JOHN DUNN

Fellow of King's College, and Reader in Politics
University of Cambridge

CAMBRIDGE UNIVERSITY PRESS

Cambridge
London   New York   Melbourne

Published by the Syndics of the Cambridge University Press
The Pitt Building, Trumpington Street, Cambridge CB2 1RP
Bentley House, 200 Euston Road, London NW1 2DB
32 East 57th Street, New York, NY 10022, USA
296 Beaconsfield Parade, Middle Park, Melbourne 3206, Australia

First published 1979

Phototypeset by
Western Printing Services Ltd, Bristol

Printed in Great Britain
at the Pitman Press, Bath

Library of Congress Cataloguing in Publication Data
Dunn, John, 1940–
Western political theory in the face of the future.
(Themes in the social sciences)
1. Political science—Europe—History. I. Title.
II. Series.
JA84.E9D86   320.5'094   78–25625
ISBN 0 521 22619 8 hard covers
ISBN 0 521 29578 5 paperback

Reproduced, printed and bound in Great Britain
at The Pitman Press, Bath

Contents

vwvwvwvwvwvwvwvwvwvwvwvwvwvwvwvwvwvwvwvwvwvwvwvwvwvwvwvw

For Sophie, William and Paul

Preface

This book asks a simple – perhaps indeed a naive – question. Do the traditions of understanding politics which have been developed in Europe over the last two and a half millennia possess any real residual capacity to direct us in the face of the world which now confronts us? Do they still exert any real imaginative or moral purchase upon this world which we, as a species, have remade so drastically? Or are they simply crazed myths clashing meaninglessly in a night which they can neither understand nor illuminate? The confidence that they do still provide such understanding and guidance is widely enough distributed in the world today, as it has been in the past. It is on open display any day of the week in Washington or Moscow, Pekin or London. But the assurance of the tone with which it is pronounced is not matched at present by the intellectual force and coherence of what is asserted. There is not, of course, anything necessarily very surprising in this state of affairs. If human beings in the past have never understood fully what was happening to the societies in which they lived, why should we expect to be privileged in our insight? If human history has been opaque to its makers thus far, why should it have become transparent to us? But unsurprising though such a condition may well be, it is not in itself necessarily any the more agreeable to experience.

What is attempted here is a sketch of some of the central anomalies of our political understanding today – in what we value politically and what we suppose to be politically possible. It is a sketch both of how these anomalies have come about and of how they now stand. As a sketch it can at best do no more than stimulate and illuminate. For those who have the courtesy and optimism to read it through and who find it neither stimulating nor illuminating (whether because they cannot believe what it argues or because they cannot understand it, or because they already know better), I can only apologize for having wasted their time. It is immodest to offer such a sketch to the public.

But it is also intellectually and perhaps even morally reprehensible, at least for those whose profession is to teach about politics, not tacitly to have such a sketch at the back of their minds – at their disposal. (While the immodesty may be mercifully rare, the unavailability of the sketch is perhaps, distressingly, more common.) The present text was written as a set of lectures for a particular audience; but it was also written out of a sense of belated embarrassment at the glib relations between a number of my own political opinions and expectations – and thus written in the first instance simply to clear my own head. The question which I have tried to answer for myself is simply whether my own conceptions of political value and possibility make sense. The answer is discouragingly indefinite, but not abjectly despondent. It would be nice to be shown how to make it unsuperstitiously more definite and more encouraging.

The text itself is written to be read continuously and without prior historical or philosophical knowledge. The footnotes are intended as guides to the pursuit of further inquiries into sundry issues discussed or, in a few cases, as justifications for some of the more flagrant formulations in the text. Earlier versions of each chapter were given as lectures whilst acting as Cecil H. & Ida Green Visiting Professor at the University of British Columbia. I am deeply grateful, to the University and to many individuals, for the extraordinary kindness and hospitality with which I was treated during the fortnight which I spent in its beautiful setting.

This book has had more and better friends than it deserves already. I owe particular debts in connection with it to Patricia Williams for her advice and kindness and to Ed Hundert for his companionship and encouragement. Once again I have trespassed grossly on the patience and the critical energies of Geoffrey Hawthorn and Quentin Skinner and once again they have encouraged me where encouragement seemed distantly permissible and made me try again where even their charity was overstretched. I only wish that the results of my further efforts were a more impressive testimony to my gratitude.

Cambridge, August 1978

1

ᘛᘛᘛᘛᘛᘛᘛᘛᘛᘛᘛᘛᘛᘛᘛᘛᘛᘛᘛᘛᘛᘛᘛᘛᘛᘛᘛᘛᘛᘛᘛᘛᘛᘛᘛᘛ

Democratic theory

'Actually, there always have to be chiefs.'

Mao Tse-Tung (6 February 1967) (quoted from Frederic Wakeman Jr, *History and Will: Philosophical Perspectives of Mao Tse-Tung's Thought*, pb. ed. Berkeley, Calif. 1975, p. 315).

We are all democrats today. Mr Callaghan and Madam Mao, Mr Brezhnev and President Amin, Mr Trudeau and even Mr Vorster. In some countries, it is true, *armies* enjoy a suzerainty which they are at pains to proclaim as temporary. And around the Persian Gulf, in Morocco and here and there in the Himalayas and South East Asia a tatty monarchy or two still adorns the map. But even these strive to ingratiate themselves as best they may as the instruments of their *people*'s purposes, tools of the *Demos*. Some monarchies are still fairly immodest both in the life styles of their royal houses and in the rhetoric of their public self-descriptions. 'Is it not passing brave to be a king/and ride in triumph through Persepolis?'[1] And nonetheless brave merely because your grandfather was no closer to being a King than – for example – Mrs Thatcher's father. But the proudest kings today, the occupants of Peacock thrones, the orchestrators of OPEC, the flushest clients of Harrods and the British armaments industry, are – and know all too well that they are – not Kings by Right Divine but kings temporarily and on sufferance, kings by permission of the People. The techniques by which monarchs today retain their thrones are technically more modern than those which Machiavelli recommended in *The Prince* four and a half centuries ago; but they are conceived in much the same disabused terms. Kings today (real kings – kings that *rule*) survive for any length of time only by a deft balance of repressive capacity and utility. Such legitimacy as they can retain even among their own

1 Christopher Marlowe, *Tamburlaine the Great*, Part I, Act 2, Scene 5, ll. 53–4 (*The Plays of Christopher Marlowe*, ed. Roma Gill, London, 1971, p. 76).

1

repressive instruments (army, secret police, state bureaucracy) depends upon their title to utility and thus in the last resort, however caricatured the claim may be in reality, it depends on their claim to represent the interests of their people.

This is all not how it used to be.

Nor, of course, is it very concretely how it now *is*, in social and political reality. To learn that all modern states claim to represent their population's interests and that almost all – all except a handful of monarchies – even claim that their political forms at present constitute (or will shortly, as soon as the emergency is over, come to do so) a government *by* the people themselves, to be told all this, is at first sight to learn little more than words. And words, as Thomas Hobbes said, 'are wise men's counters, they do but reckon by them; but they are the money of fools'.[2] Democratic theory is the moral Esperanto of the present nation-state system, the language in which all Nations are truly United, the public cant of the modern world, a dubious currency indeed – and one which only a complete imbecile would be likely to take quite at its face value, quite literally. But it is with democratic theory that it seems right to begin – not the reality of democracy, democracy as a social fact, a theme about which there being so little concrete evidence, so little social and historical reality actually to talk about, there might prove to be rather little to say. Democratic reality is certainly pretty thin on the ground.

But the intellectual origins and the historical development of the public cant of the modern world at least offers a subject to discuss which is as palpable, as historically given and as extensive as one could wish.

What *can* we reckon, then, in our sanguine wisdom from the sheer prevalence, the cosmopolitan charm of these words? If we are all democrats today in theory, *why* are we all so? And if we all used not to be – used to be nothing of the kind – how and why have we come to be so?

It will be best, perhaps, to start the historical inquiry by attempting briefly to give the flavour of the political convictions which made democracy politically unenticing in the past, either as a practical arrangement for organizing the government of a society or as a set of more abstract political values. We may take first of all a passage from a pamphlet published in London in December 1648, purportedly by King Charles himself, at that time a prisoner in the hands of the Parliamentary army at Hurst Castle on the Solent:

2 Thomas Hobbes, *Leviathan*, ed. M. Oakeshott, Oxford n.d., Part I, cap. 4, p. 22.

'There is nothing [that] can more obstruct the long hoped for peace of this Nation, than the illegal proceedings of them that presume from servants to become masters and labour to bring in democracy.'[3]

There was a social hierarchy and a legal order, with both of which democracy was incompatible. Almost two months later, on 30 January 1649, on the scaffold at Whitehall, as Charles addressed his people for the last time – or at least addressed that handful of dependable enemies among them who were all that the soldiers permitted within earshot – he restated the same theme:

'Truly I desire their liberty and freedom as much as anybody whomsoever; but I must tell you their liberty and freedom consists in having of government, those laws by which their life and their goods may be most their own. It is not for having a share in government, Sir, that is nothing pertaining to them. A subject and a sovereign are clear different things.'[4]

Charles I, of course, was an obstinate man, a man of somewhat limited imagination, and a man the limitations of whose imagination may in a sense, if a little unkindly, be said to have been responsible for his very presence on the scaffold. He was also, of course, a King himself and thus perhaps occupationally liable to be oversensitive to the categorical character of the gulf between subjects and sovereigns. And despite the excellence of his artistic taste he was hardly an outstanding exemplar of seventeenth century intellectual high culture. Even so, his views on the merits of democracy were far from historically eccentric. A little later in the century, in 1683, we find the great philosopher Leibniz, the cleverest man in seventeenth century Europe, though it must be confessed not intellectually at his most commanding when reflecting on politics, writing in a private letter to a German aristocrat about the best and most Christian form of government that: 'today there is no prince so bad that it would not be better to live under him than in a democracy'.[5]

No prince so bad. Today, no doubt, we would simply reverse the values – no prince so good that to live under him would be better than to live in a democracy. And it is clear that the enormity for the men of the seventeenth century (or at least for their rulers and the ideological

3 *His Majesty's Declaration concerning the Treaty*, cited from C. V. Wedgwood, *The Trial of Charles I*, pb. ed. London, 1964, p. 71.
4 *King Charles his Speech made upon the scaffold*, cited from Wedgwood, *Trial of Charles I*, p. 217.
5 *The Political Writings of Leibniz*, ed. Patrick Riley, Cambridge 1972, p. 186. (Leibniz was writing to Landgraf Ernst of Hesse-Rheinfels.)

apologists for their rulers) did not simply reside in the word 'democracy'. It was the idea of political authority depending at any point on the overt choice and will of the people at large which really chilled the holders of social authority in seventeenth century Europe, chilled even those, like Oliver Cromwell himself, who did not in the end shrink even from ordering the execution of their own King. Even those whose theories based political legitimacy upon the consent of the people could be expected to blench at the idea of such consent becoming too direct and too overt (and thus too blatantly reversible). The most withering early critic of John Locke, the non-juror Charles Leslie, savaged Locke for the evasiveness, the sheer disingenuousness of his theory. Reducing the consensual basis of government to a crushing absurdity, he sneered at Locke: 'Would they send men about to poll the whole nation?'[6]

Today, of course, most whole nations (or at least the adult segments of them) have been polled at some time or other. But in 1703, it is well to remember, no *whole* nation in the modern sense *had* been polled – anywhere – ever: not even half a whole adult nation, the male adult half. Nor had anyone ever so far as we know, even among the denizens of Christopher Hill's *World Turned Upside Down*,[7] proposed seriously that such promiscuous and comprehensive adult participation by both sexes and throughout the population of an entire territorial society could possibly be a sane procedure for arranging the government of that society. The Levellers in England during the Great Rebellion had, it is true, argued for something which – at least to Cromwell and Ireton, if not to Professor Macpherson[8] – sounded suspiciously like adult male

---

6 Charles Leslie, *The New Association of Those Called Moderate-Church-Men with the Modern Whigs and Fanatics . . .*, Part II, London, 1703, Appendix p. 10. The precise sense in which Locke's political theory in the *Two Treatises of Government* (1690) does base governmental legitimacy upon popular consent remains disputed. For a discussion see John Dunn, 'Consent in the Political Theory of John Locke', *The Historical Journal*, X, 2, June 1967, pp. 153–82. For the historical context of Leslie as a critic of Locke see John Dunn, 'The Politics of Locke in England and America', in J. W. Yolton (ed.), *John Locke: Problems and Perspectives*, Cambridge 1969, esp. pp. 61–4; Gordon P. Schochet, *Patriarchalism in Political Thought*, Oxford 1975, esp. pp. 221–4; Martyn P. Thompson, 'The Reception of Locke's *Two Treatises of Government* 1690–1705', *Political Studies*, XXIV, 2, June 1976, 184–91; Jeffrey M. Nelson, 'Unlocking Locke's Legacy: A Comment', *Political Studies*, XXVI, 1 March 1978, 101–8.

7 Christopher Hill, *The World Turned Upside Down*, London 1972.

8 The text of the Putney debates is conveniently available in A. S. P. Woodhouse (ed.), *Puritanism and Liberty*, London 1938. For recent dispute about the qualifications for the franchise favoured by the Leveller writers both in the Putney debates and subsequently see C. B. Macpherson, *The Political Theory of Possessive Individualism*, Oxford 1962, pp. 107–59; Keith Thomas, 'The Levellers and the Franchise', in G. E.

suffrage. They had argued their case on fairly naturalistic grounds: as Colonel Rainborough famously put it: 'really I think the poorest he that is in England hath a life to live as the greatest he'.[9] But whereas there may be little conviction to the view that what Rainborough really meant was not 'the poorest he' but rather 'the poorest economically independent agent on the market', there are no grounds for doubting that what he meant was indeed literally 'the poorest *he*' – the poorest male adult – and not as one might today put it, the poorest *person*. There were, of course, those whose rejection of seventeenth century English society and its values went still deeper than that of the Levellers, Winstanley the Digger,[10] the Ranters,[11] or the outriders of the Fifth Monarchy, eager, as they somewhat presumptuously put it, 'to help Christ to the throne of England'.[12] But none of these envisaged clearly a settled political form, whether secular or sacred, for England as a whole. None had a coherent theory, that is to say, of the character of the post-revolutionary state; and, if their critique of hierarchy was still more radical than that of the Levellers, it left them either with no coherent theory of terrestrial political action at all or else with one which (as with some other later revolutionaries) may have promised eventual freedom for all but in the meantime offered a crisply elitist doctrine of political authority for themselves.

It is, then, no simple matter even to identify a set of persons in the seventeenth century who were with any certainty convinced secular

Aylmer (ed.), *The Interregnum: the Quest for Settlement*, London 1972, pp. 57–78; Iain Hampsher-Monk, 'The Political Theory of the Levellers: Putney, Property and Professor Macpherson', *Political Studies*, XXIV, 4, December 1976, 397–422. Cromwell and Ireton's interpretation can be judged from the text of the Putney debates themselves. For an especially interesting discussion of the rationale of Leveller attitudes see now Edmund Leites, 'Conscience, Leisure and Learning: Locke and the Levellers', *Sociological Analysis*, XXXIX, 1, 1978, 36–61.

9 For Rainborough's famous speech see *Puritanism and Liberty*, p. 53; and compare Ireton's reply pp. 53–5, especially p. 53: 'Give me leave to tell you, that if you make this the rule I think you must fly for refuge to an absolute natural right, and you must deny all civil right . . . For my part, I think it no right at all.' See also Rainborough's formulations, p. 55 'any man that is born in England' and p. 56 'the meanest man in the kingdom'.

10 Hill discusses Winstanley extensively in *World Turned Upside Down* and has edited a valuable collection of his writings (Gerrard Winstanley, *The Law of Freedom and other Writings*, pb. ed. Harmondsworth 1973). A fuller (though not a complete) edition of his writings is G. H. Sabine (ed.), *The Writings of Gerrard Winstanley*, Ithaca 1941. The most extensive secondary study remains David W. Petegorsky, *Left-Wing Democracy in the English Civil War*, London, 1940.

11 For the Ranters see especially Hill, *The World Turned Upside Down*.

12 as John Simpson urged his congregation at All Hallows the Great from prison at Windsor. See B. S. Capp, *The Fifth Monarchy Men*, London 1972, p. 102.

democrats. Democracy was notoriously a form of political regime which had played a major role in the history of Ancient Greece. But Ancient Greece was distant by virtually two millennia and no one at all in the seventeenth century as far as we know, identified their *own* political values by *calling* themselves 'democrats'. As a term of political self-description 'democrat' does not reappear in any western European language until the late eighteenth century and when it does appear, it appears in political antithesis to the word 'aristocrat'.[13] The late eighteenth century assault on the closed privileged caste order[14] of the post-feudal Ancien Regime, in Europe as a whole and of course above all in France, was responsible for the resurrection of the term 'democrat' as a term of political self-identification. Until the 1780s it was semantically possible (and politically quite effective) to describe the political principles or aspirations of one's opponents as 'democratic' or 'democratical' (one can find Boswell, for example, doing so[15]); but no one, even the most radical, would describe their *own* political principles or aspirations firmly in these terms.

It is not difficult to explain why this should have been so. Democracy was a Greek word, a secular word and an intellectual's word. Such radical politics as one can find in Europe in the seventeenth and even for most of the eighteenth century, was either explicitly sacred or else populist and prescriptive in tone, fighting as the Levellers did for the restoration of what they thought to be *traditional* popular rights, the liberties of free-born Englishmen, to cast off the Norman Yoke of

13 R. R. Palmer, 'Notes on the Use of the Word "Democracy" 1789–1799', *Political Science Quarterly*, LXVIII, 2 June 1953, 203–26.
14 See e.g. Emmanuel Joseph Sieyès, *What is the Third Estate?* (tr. M. Blondel), London 1963, esp. p. 104: 'To think only in terms of wholesomeness, what kind of society is it in which you *lose caste* if you work? Where to consume is honourable but to produce is vile? and p. 177: 'Caste is the right word. It describes a class of men who although they lack functions and usefulness enjoy privileges attaching to their person by the mere fact of birth. It is truly a nation apart.' And see J. Q. C. Mackrell, *The Attack on 'Feudalism' in Eighteenth Century France*, London 1973. For the very late date at which this assault was mounted politically on at all a broad front see Colin Lucas, 'Nobles, Bourgeois and the Origins of the French Revolution', *Past and Present*, Vol. LX, August 1973, 84–126; and George Taylor, 'Revolutionary and Non-revolutionary content in the *Cahiers* of 1789', *French Historical Studies*, VII, 4, Fall 1972, 479–502.
15 See e.g. James Boswell on Johnson's critic Joseph Towers: 'I am willing to do justice to the merit of Dr Towers, of whom I will say, that although I abhor his Whiggish democratical notions and propensities, (for I will not call them principles,) I esteem him as an ingenious, knowing, and very convivial man' (James Boswell, *The Life of Dr Johnson*, 1775), London 1906 ed., Vol. 1, p. 529. For a balanced view of Johson's own political attitudes see Donald J. Greene, *The Politics of Samuel Johnson*, New Haven 1960. Johnson himself freely employed the word 'Whig' as a term of abuse. ('Where you see a Whig you see a rascal' etc. See e.g. Greene, *op. cit.*, pp. 18–19.)

William the Bastard,[16] or else they were very firmly intellectual indeed and set either in the language of autocratic reform or of explicitly Utopian moral aspiration. The populist politics were necessarily very firmly vernacular – Anglo-Saxon at all costs as opposed to Greek. The intellectuals' politics by contrast were either very firmly autocratic, committed, like reforming ministers such as Turgot,[17] to the effective concentration of power in the hands of the royal government. Or else such intellectuals were intractable moralists, deeply pessimistic about the very possibility of restoring or creating a good society. Where it figures in the writings of any of these men, democracy figures as a theoretical term for a peculiarly accident-prone form of state, necessarily socially divided, exceptionally exigent in the type of political culture (the dedicated public virtue of its citizen body) which it required in order to survive at all – and radically unsuited both politically and militarily to compete against the modern state forms of the time, the absolute monarchies of the West. If there was one wholly undisputed conclusion of academic political theory in the mid eighteenth century, the entire way across the political spectrum, it was that democracy as a distinct form of political regime had gone and gone to stay.[18]

We can catch the flavour of this assurance best perhaps from the comments of the greatest mid eighteenth century theorist of the European Ancien Regime, the Bordeaux magistrate, Charles Louis de Secondat, Baron de Montesquieu, on the fate of the Levellers' political ambitions. In his great book *De l'Esprit des Loix*, published in 1748, Montesquieu noted coolly:

'It was a fine spectacle last century to watch the helpless efforts of the English to establish democracy among themselves. Since those who

16 See Christopher Hill, *Puritanism and Revolution*, pb. ed. London 1962, cap. 3, 'The Norman Yoke'. And see from the Putney debates, *Puritanism and Liberty*, p. 52, p. 120 (Cowling), p. 122 (Wildman).
17 Franklin L. Ford, *Sword and Robe*, Cambridge, Mass. 1953, esp. cap. 12; and Peter Gay, *Voltaire's Politics: The Poet as Realist*, Princeton 1959. For Turgot's career see Douglas Dakin, *Turgot and the Ancien Regime in France*, London 1939. And for a terse summary of his attitudes: '*Votre Majesté, tant qu'elle ne s'écartera de la justice, peut se regarder comme un législateur absolu*' (quoted from Georges Weulersse, *La Physiocratie sous les ministères de Turgot et de Necker (1774–1781)*, Paris 1950, p. 111.
18 Franco Venturi, *Utopia and Reform in the Enlightenment*, Cambridge 1971, caps. 1–3. There is an interesting, but in the end somewhat equivocal, defence of the view that Montesquieu conceived democracy as a still viable state form in Nannerl O. Keohane, 'Virtuous Republics and Glorious Monarchies: Two Models in Montesquieu's Political Thought', *Political Studies*, XX, 4, December 1972, pp. 383–96. Keohane establishes Montesquieu's indubitable esteem for democratic republicanism but passes a little lightly over the issue of his judgement of its viability within the state system of eighteenth century Europe.

were taking part in public life lacked virtue . . . the government changed incessantly. The astonished people searched for democracy and could find it nowhere. In the end, after many movements, shocks and jolts, they were forced to come to rest in just the same form of government as they had earlier proscribed.'[19]

And so, he implied, it was bound to be – so, any competent political theorist could have told them before they had even started.

But if this dismissal of the viability of democracy as a political form was a fair summary of a European intellectual consensus which reached back at least to the Principate of Augustus, it was a consensus which disappeared with surprising speed between 1776 and 1850 in Europe itself.

Again we may take a single example. A young French aristocrat, Alexis de Tocqueville, a deep admirer of Montesquieu, was visiting England for the first time in 1833, a year or so after his return from a trip to America which he was to immortalize a few years later, in 1835 and 1840, by publishing the most impressive single interpretative study of the United States and what is still probably the most important study of democratic values ever written, *Democracy in America*. On leaving London early in 1833 de Tocqueville was trying to sum up his impressions and to assess the probability of England's succumbing shortly to revolution. On the whole, he thought not. But he was confident that the English aristocracy were bound to go under, for a number of reasons.

'The first,' he said, 'results from the general movement common to humanity the world over in our time. The century is primarily democratic. Democracy is like a rising tide; it only recoils to come back with greater force, and soon one sees that for all its fluctuations it is always gaining ground. The immediate future of European society is completely democratic; this can in no way be doubted. Thus the common people in England are beginning to get the idea that they, too, can take a part in government. The class placed immediately above it, but which has not yet played a notable part in the course of events, especially shows this ill-defined urge for growth and for power, and is becoming more numerous and more restless day by day. Furthermore the discomforts and real poverty suffered in England in our time, give birth to ideas and excite passions which would perhaps have long continued to sleep if the State had been prosperous.

19 Montesquieu, *L'Esprit des Loix*, ed. J. Brethe de la Gressaye, Paris 1950, Vol. 1, p. 57. (Bk III, cap. 3; and see the *Pensée* on the same subject quoted by the editor, *op. cit.*, Vol. 1, p. 250.)

'So a gradual development of the democratic principle must follow from the irresistible march of events. Daily some further privilege of the aristocracy comes under attack; it is a slow war waged about details, but infallibly in time it will bring the whole edifice down.'[20]

It is striking that de Tocqueville, an aristocrat and a man living in the European society with the deepest experience of political revolution, still, even after his American tour, saw the political meaning of democracy as essentially the repudiation of the feudal past, the triumph of the non-privileged over the aristocrats, the victory of the Third Estate.

In 1833 'democracy' was a European word and a rather parochial and chronologically distant European experience precariously transposed onto the European transition from the Ancien Regime to the post-revolutionary modern state, or, if you will but in terms which de Tocqueville would *not* have used, the political component of the European transition from feudalism to capitalism. But 'democracy' was not to remain a privately European word or conception for very much longer. By 1900 the consolidation of the world market which Marx saw as the historical task of the bourgeoisie, and the invasive thrust of western imperialism, had brought democracy – as a term and an idea, if hardly as a concrete experience – to the most unlikely places. Democracy was a Greek political invention which for the Greeks never really breached the barriers of the Greek cultural world: a form of government which even its adherents supposed to be fit by and large only for Greeks – and by no means a form which they would have thought of proffering wholesale to the barbarians. On the whole the Greeks were tolerably convinced cultural bigots.[21] But they were, of course, both militarily and politically, in the long run remarkably unsuccessful cultural bigots,[22] falling an easy victim to the expanding power of Rome. By 1900 the Greek concept 'democracy' had penetrated even to the Central Kingdom, the Celestial Empire of China. The Chinese, by contrast, were the most successful cultural bigots whom world history has yet seen, defining the world which they knew and the political and cultural transactions between themselves and the rest of it resolutely in

20 Alexis de Tocqueville, *Journeys to England and Ireland*, ed. J. P. Mayer, tr. G. Lawrence & K. Mayer, London 1958 (last impressions of England, 7 Sept. 1833), pp. 67–8.
21 For a synoptic survey of the limits of this conviction throughout Greek intellectual history see H. C. Baldry, *The Unity of Mankind in Greek Thought*, Cambridge 1965.
22 For a witty and penetrating discussion of the relations between the practical failure and the cultural obtuseness see Arnaldo Momigliano, *Alien Wisdom: The Limits of Hellenization*, Cambridge 1975 (particularly severe on the Greeks' performance as linguists).

their own terms and with themselves at its centre for almost two thousand years.[23] Chinese culture *was* culture. The culture of everywhere else was savage custom, fit material for anthropologists, if the Chinese had supposed savages to be intrinsically interesting enough even to merit study. On the whole European words proved exceptionally difficult to translate into Chinese. But the one word which travelled perfectly from fifth century Athens to nineteenth century China and provided transparent understanding on its arrival was the word 'barbarian'. For the Chinese, Europeans were paradigm barbarians; and the thorny problems of learning to handle them were approached by courses in barbarian studies. On 6 October 1897, Liang Ch'i Ch'ao, a leading mandarin striving for political influence at court and a deep and diligent student of the barbarians,[24] published an article in a Shanghai periodical, *Chinese Progress* (a title which was in itself unpleasantly close to a contradiction in terms).

'When the cycles of the world are about to move,' he wrote, 'into the period of universal peace, it is not something restricted to the West, nor something that China can avoid. I know that in less than a hundred years, all five continents will be under the rule of the people, and our China will not be able to continue unchanged. This is a law of things which nobody can contravene.

'Among the Westerners, the cycle of many rulers has been long, and that of one ruler short; as for China, the cycle of many rulers was short, and that of one ruler long . . . as for the future, all will become democracies.'[25]

And so, after their fashion, a mere eighty years later, they almost all have. But why have they done so? And in becoming so, what exactly is it that they have now become?

There are in essence two rather simple reasons why they have done so; or perhaps it would be neater to think of it as a single reason which can be expressed in two different ways. The first of these was well expressed by the youthful Karl Marx in his critical commentary on the not especially democratic theory of the modern state advanced by Hegel.

23 See Joseph R. Levenson, *Confucian China and its Modern Fate*, 3 vols., London 1958–65; Joseph R. Levenson, *Liang Ch'i-Ch'ao and the Mind of Modern China*, pb. ed. Berkeley, Calif. 1959; John K. Fairbank (ed.), *The Chinese World Order*, Cambridge, Mass. 1968.
24 See Levenson, *Liang Ch'i-Ch'ao*; Hao Chang, *Liang Ch'i-Ch'ao and Intellectual Transition in China 1890–1907*, Cambridge, Mass. 1971; Philip C. Huang, *Liang Ch'i-Ch'ao and Modern Chinese Liberalism*, Seattle 1972.
25 Don C. Price, *Russia and the Roots of the Chinese Revolution, 1896—1911*, Cambridge, Mass. 1974, pp. 26–7, 229–30.

'Democracy,' Marx wrote, 'is the resolved mystery of all constitutions. Here the constitution . . . is returned to its real ground, actual man, the actual people, and established as its own work. The constitution appears as what it is, the free product of men.'[26]

The resolved mystery of *all* constitutions.

The demos of modern democratic theory is supposedly all the people or at least all the adult people. And modern states prefer to claim that it is indeed the people as a whole or certainly their great majority that actually hold power within them, because they can think of no better title to rule over the people than the free choice of the people themselves. Nor, if the claim were indeed valid, would there be much reason to suppose them wrong in this conviction.

The second way of putting this simple thought attempts to explain not the *present* prevalence of democratic verbiage, but rather the transition from past *to* present: from virtually absent to overwhelmingly dominant. The cause of this transition in political language is seen then as a broad general shift in human culture from pre-modern to modern society, the process which Max Weber, following Schiller, christened the 'Disenchantment of the World'.[27] The modern political idiom, at face, is rational, universal, unsuperstitious, perhaps a shade mechanical. The pre-modern political idiom was local, superstitious, perhaps affectively denser and more immediate. The transition was a triumph of rationality over diffuse sentiment – to quote Marx once again, 'a mystery resolved'.

To the first of the two queries, then, we can present a simple and rather encouraging answer. Verbally speaking, we are all democrats today because so we transparently ought to be. Democratic theory is the public cant of the modern world; and cant is the verbal medium of hypocrisy; and hypocrisy is the tribute which vice pays to virtue. All states today profess to be democracies because a democracy is what it is virtuous for a state to be.

But what *is* a democracy?

And what have almost all modern states thus become, in virtue of

---

26 Karl Marx, *Critique of Hegel's Philosophy of Right* (tr. A. Jolin & J. O'Malley. Ed J. O'Malley), Cambridge 1970, pp. 29–30. And see also *op. cit.*, p. 30: 'Democracy is the essence of every political constitution, socialized man under the form of a particular constitution of the state. It stands related to other constitutions as the genus to its species . . . Democracy is *human existence*, while in the other political forms man has only *legal* existence,' and p. 31: 'all forms of the state have democracy for their truth, and for that reason are false to the extent that they are not democracy'.

27 Max Weber, *The Protestant Ethic and Spirit of Capitalism* (tr. Talcott Parsons), pb. ed. New York 1958, pp. 105, 221–2.

proclaiming themselves to be democracies? The answer, here too, is fairly simple. But it is appreciably less encouraging. At this level what democracy is is a highly desirable label for which the exceedingly heterogeneous class of modern states show a strong predilection when they come to describe themselves in public. It would be naive to think of it as giving a very helpful descriptive résumé of any particular factual situation. Nor, despite the eagerness of sundry types of modern state to monopolize the criteria of application for the word 'democracy', would it make much sense any longer to presume that any single grouping – say the 'Western Democracies' of the NATO alliance or the 'People's Democracies' of eastern Europe – has a valid claim to its exclusive use.[28]

Democracy, then, may once have been the name of a particular form of regime, a very particular form indeed. But now it is the name for the good intentions of states or perhaps for the good intentions which their rulers would like us to believe that they possess.

But surely there must be somewhat more theory to democratic theory than the simple preference of rulers for being thought well-intentioned? And so indeed there is. Putting it unkindly, it is possible to sum up the additional component fairly briskly: democratic theory specifies not merely that the rulers of states today have good intentions, insofar as they are democrats (in itself a claim of widely varying truth no doubt); but also that they claim to have a particular sort of intention which they cannot, even in principle, *act out* in reality.

In the days when democracy was the name for a highly distinct form of political regime, democracies were states which took the political component of citizen equality rather seriously. Modern states, by contrast, however seriously they may take social or economic equality (and there are, of course, many which take either or both a great deal more seriously than ancient Athens did) are precluded by their very structure from giving more than token recognition to the ideal of political equality. Modern state structures concentrate power to a degree which no ancient state could have begun to emulate and to a degree that fifth and fourth century BC Athenians, for example, would

28 In this sense there is considerable force to Professor Macpherson's insistence on the plurality of contemporary theories of democracy (C. B. Macpherson, *The Real World of Democracy*, Oxford 1966). But the absence of a legitimate monopoly in the use of the term does not make it satisfactory to abandon, as Macpherson does in practice, the use of any determinate political criteria for applying the category 'democracy'. (See John Dunn, 'Democracy Unretrieved; or the Political Theory of Professor Macpherson', *British Journal of Political Science*, IV, 4, October 1974, 489–99.)

have considered a complete negation of democracy.[29] Of course, not all fifth or fourth century BC Athenians would have regarded a complete negation of democracy as at all a bad thing. But those Athenians who would have called themselves democrats would certainly have regretted it; and we can best begin our consideration of the positive components of democratic theory by considering briefly what they *would* have felt to be a proper democracy.

The conventional way of marking this distinction, at least since the eighteenth century, is to contrast direct democracy, the ancient sort, with representative democracy, the modern variety. In itself, this may sound anodyne enough. One can be represented in courts by lawyers or in business dealings by those whom one has empowered to act on one's behalf. Why not in politics too?[30] And might not representative democracy be indeed in many ways an *improvement* on direct democracy? Who wouldn't rather be represented in a tricky court case by a skilled lawyer whom they had selected for themselves, rather than having to trust to their own unaided wits and a mere smattering of legal knowledge? Such thoughts certainly occurred to Tom Paine, for example, as he set himself to vindicate the French revolutionaries against Burke's sneers:

'Simple Democracy,' he said, 'was society governing itself without the aid of secondary means [a prospect perhaps a little like the withered away state?] By ingrafting representation upon Democracy, we arrive at a system of Government capable of embracing and confederating all the various interests and every extent of territory and population; and that also with advantages as much superior to hereditary Government, as the Republic of Letters is to hereditary literature.

'It is on this system that the American Government is founded [a state of affairs in which Paine took some legitimate personal pride]. It is representation ingrafted upon Democracy . . . What Athens was in miniature, America will be in magnitude. The one was the wonder of the ancient world; the other is becoming the admiration, the model of the present. It is the easiest of all the forms of Government to be understood and the most eligible in practice, and excludes at once the

29 For the record of Athenian democratic achievement see especially M. I. Finley, *Democracy Ancient and Modern*, London 1973; M. I. Finley, 'Athenian Demagogues', *Past and Present*, XXI, 1962, 3–24; Pierre Vidal-Nacquet, 'Tradition de la démocratie grecque', in Finley, *Démocratie antique et démocratie moderne*, Paris 1976, pp. 7–44; A. H. M. Jones, *Athenian Democracy*, Oxford 1957.
30 See Hanna F. Pitkin, *The Concept of Representation*, pb. ed. Berkeley, Calif. 1972, cap. 6: 'Representing as "Acting For"': The Analogies'.

ignorance and insecurity of the hereditary mode, and the inconveni-
ence of the simple Democracy.

'It is impossible to conceive a system of Government capable of
acting over such an extent of territory, and such a circle of interests, as
is immediately produced by the operation of representation. France,
great and populous as it is, is but a spot in the capaciousness of the
system. It is preferable to simple Democracy even in small territories.
Athens, by representation, would have *outrivalled* her own Democracy.'[31]

Direct democracy, then, in Paine's view was simply an ineffective
and inconvenient mechanism for achieving social goals which could be
achieved under any circumstances more effectively and more conveniently by a system of representative democracy. The scale of modern states precludes direct democracy as a mode of organizing a central
government. But this is a gain, not a cost, for the moderns, since it
merely rendered a necessity what would in any case have been a
convenience.

Paine, of course, in a fairly simple sense did not *know* what he was
talking about, there being little representative national democracy for
him to assess the workings of at the time – outside the United States of
America[32] – then as now an unsound imaginative basis on which to
form judgements of the political prospects of most societies in the
world. Some three quarters of a century later even a less simply
populist political thinker, like John Stuart Mill, had grasped the disadvantages of representation from a populist perspective. Mill's *Considerations on Representative Government* is a highly ambivalent work, very
confident, as one would expect a civil servant to be, of the professional
character of bureaucratic work and the consequent folly of government
by open meeting[33] – but also (and perhaps even *equally*) self-conscious

31 Thomas Paine, *The Rights of Man, Part II* (1792), Everyman ed. London 1915, pp. 176–7
(emphasis added).
32 For the extent of democratic development in America by 1791 see J. R. Pole, *Political
Representation in England and the Origins of the American Republic*, London 1966.
33 John Stuart Mill, *Considerations on Representative Government*, Everyman ed. London
1910. On bureaucracy as a functional prerequisite for political rationality in modern
societies see pp. 232–4; p. 335 ('the entire business of government is skilled employment'). On the central role of political participation as a value see pp. 207–9,
217–18, 243, 278–9. On the difficulty of stretching participation beyond the *polis* see
pp. 179–80, esp. 180 ('the newspaper press, the real equivalent, though not in all
respects an adequate one, of the Pnyx and the Forum'). For a valuable discussion of
Mill's attitudes towards bureaucracy see Alan Ryan, 'Utilitarianism and Bureaucracy:
the Views of J. S. Mill', in Gillian Sutherland (ed.), *Studies in the Growth of Nineteenth
Century Government*, London 1972, pp. 33–62.

about the costs of political rationalization for the participation and public commitments of the mass of individual citizens. Mill certainly did not suppose (as Marx at times appears to have done) that large-scale bureaucracy could be dispensed with in modern society. But he did realize that its indispensable presence had made drastic inroads into the very possibility of meaningful political participation for the majority of citizens. The only remedy which he saw for this effective exclusion (and it was a remedy which he himself *admitted* to be an inadequate one) was open debate in the newspaper press, a feeble substitute for the Athens hillside on which the assembled people decided the political commitments of the Athenian state.

Considered purely mechanically, there can really be no doubt at all that representative democracy *does* have some advantages over direct democracy, the most striking of which is that it saves a prodigious amount of time. But it does so, of course, at a cost; and the most striking of its costs is the extent to which it diminishes the political power of individual citizens in comparison with their power in a direct democracy. Power and rule are in the first instance terms of agency. The literal meaning of democracy is simply the rule of the people, the *demos*. In fourth century Athens, the composition of the *demos*, the specification of who actually belonged within its ranks and who was excluded from them, looks more than a little restrictive when compared with the citizen bodies of any modern states except the Union of South Africa: no women at all, none, naturally, of the rather large population of slaves, very few even of those among the resident population of Athens, the metics, who had not been Athenian citizens by birth: only Athenian adult males, almost all of solidly Athenian descent.[34] But if the democratic regime in Athens was narrow by modern standards in its citizen body, it was democratic in its political institutions to a degree that is hard for the citizen of a modern state even to comprehend. Demographically the Athenian *demos* was indeed not a half nor a quarter of the people of Athens. But unlike the punctiliously expanded *demos* of modern states, it is no idle euphem-

34 Cf. the studies cited in note 29 above. For the changing composition of the Athenian *demos* and the different criteria of citizenship on which it was based see C. Hignett, *A History of the Athenian Constitution to the End of the Fifth Century BC*, Oxford 1952, pp. 79, 84, 98, 117–23, 133–4, 136–7, 232. For the general definition of citizenship in Greek society see Aristotle, *Politics*, Bk III, 1, 2 and 5 (*Aristotle's Politics III & IV*, tr. Richard Robinson, Oxford 1962, pp. 1–6, 15–17). For an illuminating discussion of just what citizenship implied in practice see M. I. Finley, 'The Freedom of the Citizen in the Greek World', *TAΛANTA*, VII, 1975/76, pp. 1–23.

ism to claim that the Athenian *demos ruled, held* political power in Athens and exercised it by their actions. Modern states almost all have a legislature and *all* have an executive with direct control over professional forces of coercion and mostly have a third body, an electorate, which at intervals of some years confers by its performance some purported measure of legitimacy on legislature and executive. These rituals, where they are still observed, are not without meaning; and in some places they even contribute to deciding who is going to make up the legislature or the executive. But it does seem a little strained to describe them as instances of *ruling*. In the days of the Septennial Act, Jean-Jacques Rousseau unkindly sneered, the English were free once every seven years.[35] Now the score on this reckoning would be about once in four years. One day's rule in four years has very much the air of a placebo – or at best of an irregular modern Saturnalia.

But in Athens there was virtually no continuing professional bureaucracy – just for the discharge of a small number of purely routine tasks.[36] There was almost no professional apparatus of coercion – only a small slave police force. There was no distinct continuing executive, no professional judiciary and no professional legislature. Some politically important Athenian public officials were elected annually by the citizen body, a practice regarded as somewhat undemocratic in spirit because it favoured the wealthy and the culturally advantaged against the poorer citizens. But the nearest body to a continuing executive, the Council, was selected by lot from the citizen body as a whole; and any citizen was quite likely to serve on it at least once in his adult life. All important trials were held before popular courts, the members of which were also picked by lot. And, most important of all, any binding public decision of the Athenian state, the making of an alliance, the declaration of war, the passing of any law, was enacted by the popular assembly of the Athenian citizen body as a whole, meeting regularly or in emergency session for the purpose. In the fourth century, attendance at the Assembly (as with jury service or the discharge of the various magistracies) was *paid*, so that no Athenian citizen should have their political rights eroded by the cost of exercising them. In this Assembly those who spoke better or who were more skilful at ingratiating themselves with their fellow citizens were, as Plato bitterly complained, more influential than those who spoke worse or who were

35 Jean-Jacques Rousseau, *Du Contrat Social*, Bk 111, cap. XV (*Political Writings*, ed. C. E. Vaughan, Oxford 1962, II, p. 96).
36 See Jones, *Athenian Democracy*, esp. pp. 99–108.

16

politically tactless. But Athenian citizens, every single one of them able to be present on the particular occasion, enjoyed not merely equality before the law (as we ourselves do today) but something much more spectacular in the way of equality – what they called *isegoria*, an equal right to be heard in the sovereign assembly of the state before public decisions were taken.[37]

Of course such a right was more *use* to those who were glamorous and spoke well – like Alcibiades – than it might have been to ourselves or than it presumably was to Plato. Even the most direct democracy cannot remove the differences between men, cannot render them politically identical. For the Greeks, as for any sane group of persons, some men's political opinions amply deserve their lack of influence over the political opinions of others. What democracy could do, where it prevailed, was simply to give to its citizens an equal right to get themselves heard before major political decisions were taken. Such equality of right did not, as Plato and Thucydides were at pains to point out,[38] guarantee that the ensuing decisions were wise or generally advantageous. (No political procedure can offer such a guarantee.) But it did give the citizens an equality of right – and with this equality, at least the *claim* on the part of the community at large to a corresponding equality of obligation.[39] If a modern state chooses to go to war and conscripts its male population for the purpose (a right which no modern state has forgone in bulk), its citizens are seldom consulted on the matter.[40] But

37 See Finley, *Democracy Ancient and Modern*, pp. 18–19. Even Herodotus, in many ways a strikingly cosmopolitan judge, seems to have attributed the Greek defeat of the Persians in part to the cultural superiority exhibited in the Greek commitment to *isegoria* (see Momigliano, *Alien Wisdom*, pp. 130–3).

38 Almost all the ablest commentators on Athenian politics who have come down to us were bigoted opponents of the democracy. Plato's *Republic* and Thucydides' *History of the Peloponnesian War* are both much more than anti-democratic political tracts. But as critiques of the moral limitations of democracy in operation they have never been surpassed in force and urgency.

39 Cf. Peter Singer, *Democracy and Disobedience*, Oxford 1973.

40 One twentieth century instance in which an electorate has been consulted by referenda not once but twice on the acceptability of conscription (in this case, for military service overseas) occurred during the First World War in Australia. The outcome involved the fall of a government, the rejection of such conscription for a considerable period and a devastating split in the Australian Federal Labour Party. The political passions aroused during the episode have been re-evoked more recently in the course of debates over the legitimacy of Australian collaboration with the United States in South Vietnam. For a variety of perspectives on the causation and significance of the episode see Ian Turner, '1914–1919', in Francis C. Crowley (ed.), *A New History of Australia*, Melbourne 1974, pp. 312–56 & bibliography pp. 581–2; Ian Turner, *Industrial Labour and Politics: The Dynamics of the Labour Movement in Eastern Australia, 1900–1921*, Canberra 1965; K. S. Inglis, 'Conscription in Peace and War,

Athens could not *go* to war, could not demand that any of its citizens risk their lives for it in war, without securing the agreement of the assembled *demos* to do so. And no Athenian citizen could be required to go off to fight for his country and perhaps to die for it, without having at least the formal opportunity to address his fellow citizens on the merits of the venture before he did so. In the age of anti-missile missiles the political form of such symmetry between citizen right and citizen obligation beggars the imagination.

The timespan over which this paradoxical political vision has beset the western imagination is not an enormously long one. It goes back perhaps to Rousseau and it reaches up to the present – a distance of a little over two centuries since western Europeans began to wish with some urgency to live democratically and began to suspect that such a life might now in practice be impossible. The key image is still that of Rousseau, of each individual uniting himself with all and yet remaining as free as before;[41] and the two major grounds for pessimism about the prospects for success are still those which Rousseau outlined in his *Discourse on the Origins of Inequality among Men* and in the *Social Contract* itself. The first of these grounds, the incompatibility between drastic social differentiation and above all economic inequality on the one hand and political equality on the other has never been more forcefully expressed than it was by Rousseau. The inequality of reward is easier to modify than the social division of labour is to reverse. Equality of consumption may be, as the incomparable Joseph Stalin put it, 'a reactionary petty-bourgeois absurdity worthy of some primitive sect of ascetics'.[42] But its absurdity certainly falls well short of that of a modern society in which all persons in fact do identical work. In *The German Ideology* Marx wrote blithely of how in communist society it will be

1911–1945', in Roy Forward & Bob Reece (eds.), *Conscription in Australia*, St Lucia, Queensland 1968, pp. 22–65; Patrick Weller (ed.), *Caucus Minutes 1901–1949*, (sc. Of the Australian Federal Parliamentary Labour Party), Carlton, Victoria 1975, Vols. 1 & 2, index *sub* conscription. There is a biography of the protagonist of conscription, Premier William Morris Hughes up to the year 1914: Laurence F. Fitzhardinge, *William Morris Hughes: A Political Biography*, Vol. I, Sydney 1964.

41 'Trouver une forme d'association qui défende et protège de toute la force commune, la personne et les biens de chaque associé, et par laquelle chacun, s'unissant à tous, n'obéisse pourtant qu'à lui-même, et reste aussi libre qu'auparavant' (*Du Contrat Social*, Bk 1, cap. VI; *Political Writings*, ed. Vaughan, II, p. 32).

42 Report to the Seventeenth Party Congress of the CPSU, 26 January 1934 (J. V. Stalin, *Works*, Vol. XIII, Moscow 1955, p. 361; and see generally pp. 361–4: 'every Leninist knows, if he is a real Leninist, that equalisation in the sphere of requirements and personal, everyday life is a reactionary petty-bourgeois absurdity worthy of some primitive sect of ascetics, but not a socialist society organized on Marxist lines').

made possible 'for me to do one thing today and another tomorrow, to hunt in the morning, fish in the afternoon, rear cattle in the evening, criticize after dinner, just as I have a mind, without ever becoming hunter, fisherman, shepherd or critic'.[43] It sounds a charmingly pastoral existence (if one which might prove difficult to practice in Metropolitan Tokyo or central London). But what, as a modern consumer, would one feel if left at the mercy of someone who was dentist in the morning, architect in the afternoon, kidney surgeon in the evening and corporation dustperson after dinner, without ever becoming constricted within the roles? Redness may be more important than expertness;[44] but a political future which promised to dispense with expertise would be necessarily an idiot's promise or a promise made in the deepest bad faith.

The second of Rousseau's grounds for pessimism about the possibility of democratic life is also related to the progress of social differentiation. But it is not identical with this. The Greek *Polis*, as Rousseau seems to have believed and as Hegel underlined with even greater emphasis, stood in a much more dominant position towards its citizens than does a modern state. The 'principle of subjectivity'[45] as Hegel

43 Karl Marx & Frederick Engels, *The German Ideology* (1845–46), *Collected Works of Marx and Engels*, Vol. V, London 1976, p. 47.

44 For the tension between redness and expertise in Chinese political values see the Supplement to the second edition of Franz Schurmann, *Ideology and Organization in Communist China*, pb. ed. Berkeley, Calif. 1968, pp. 503–92. The Great Proletarian Cultural Revolution represented the most remarkable twentieth century attempt to reverse the structural social inequality generated by the division of labour. It is a controversial question how far any such attempt necessarily weakens the productive capacities of a population. But it seems a reasonable presumption at present that the motivation of the political initiator of the process was more concerned with moral and cultural aspects of social existence than with the effort to increase production in the short term. (For a mildly surprising – and fleeting – espousal of a comparable conception of the appropriateness of a uniform distribution of hours of physical labour and study throughout a population irrespective of their status or role see John Locke, 'Labour', quoted in Dunn, *Political Thought of Locke*, p. 231 n. 6; and note the abrupt recoil at the thought that such a distribution might 'seem not fair nor sufficiently to keep up the distinction that ought to be in the ranks of men', *op. cit.*, pp. 231–2 n. 7.) It also seems a reasonable judgement at present that the reversal of the Cultural Revolution indicates not the economic inefficiency of the localization of control over production which it created but rather the political fragility of any such localization of power within a modern state: its dependence for initial licence on the consent of centralized forces of coercion and its inability to protect itself against the reimposition of effective central control (and 'the distinction that ought to be in the ranks of men' which has in due course accompanied this) once that licence was revoked.

45 See G. W. F. Hegel, *The Philosophy of History*, tr. J. Sibree, pb. ed. New York 1956, Part IV, Section III, pp. 412–57; *The Philosophy of Right*, tr. T. M. Knox, Oxford 1942, especially para. 260, pp. 160–1 ('The principle of modern states has prodigious

called it (or Christianity, as Rousseau more narrowly saw it)[46] had given to modern men a much more inflated sense of their own importance as individuals. The ancients had seen their community as a focus of value, an entity the significance of which dwarfed that of their own lives as individuals. Modern men saw their communities, rather, as incidental conveniences and played them for what could be got out of them. Rousseau's solution to the dilemma of political legitimacy in the modern world was a Utopia, small enough in scale and undifferentiated enough in social composition to be a real moral focus for the lives of its members – and a Utopia in which citizens would be reared to set the good of the community above their own individual advantages. Such a community, he recognized clearly enough, was no longer viable in the geopolitical and military ecology of eighteenth century Europe.[47]

Some eighty years later Karl Marx saw this same moral rift between individual and community as precluding the development of an integrated political society. But he had a simpler and more encouraging theory of how this rift had come about – and a theory which claimed to show how the rift could be mended. The capitalist mode of production which had widened the rift to its fullest extent and which set every individual existentially and spiritually against each other, at one another's throats, had begun to create its political and moral – and in due course economic – antithesis, the new and morally solidary community of the industrial working class. The objective situation of the proletariat compelled it to become Communist.[48] In retrospect the judgement that the capitalist mode of production and the enormous

strength and depth because it allows the principle of subjectivity to progress to its culmination in the extreme of self-subsistent personal particularity, and yet at the same time brings it back to the substantive unity and so maintains this unity in the principle of subjectivity itself') and the addition to para. 260, p. 280; *Early Theological Writings*, tr. T. M. Knox, pb. ed. New York 1961, 'The Spirit of Christianity and its Fate', esp. pp. 205–13.

46 Rousseau's profound ambivalence about this impact and his hostility to the specifically political implications of Christianity both as an organized Church and as an individual ethic are eloquently described in Judith Shklar, *Men and Citizens: A Study of Rousseau's Social Theory*, Cambridge 1968, pp, 114–26. For a very strong statement of the demerits of Christianity in both of these guises ('la religion du prêtre' and 'la religion de l'homme . . . celui de l'Évangile'), see *Du Contrat Social*, Bk IV, cap. 8, *Political Writings*, ed. C. E. Vaughan, Vol. II, pp. 128–31.

47 See e.g. *Du Contrat Social*, Bk I, cap. 9 n., Bk III, cap. 4, cap. 15, *Political Writings*, ed. Vaughan, II, p. 38n, 72–4, 95–8 (but cf. Vaughan's note, pp. 134–5) and Rousseau's letter to the Marquis de Mirabeau, 26 July 1767, *Political Writings*, II, 159–62. To speak of it as a *solution* to the problem of legitimacy is in any case perhaps to employ too strong a term – see Shklar, *Men and Citizens*.

48 For the classic statement see *Manifesto of the Communist Party* (1848), Karl Marx &

expansion in productive forces which this has generated have indeed been responsible for the genesis of modern individualism and the radically instrumental conception of community which this implies has worn fairly well. What has not worn at all well, by contrast, indeed what now looks sentimental and self-deceptive, is the judgement that the development of modern capitalism (or indeed of modern socialism in industrial countries) is bound to generate a new and morally integrated mass community, the moral authority of which will be accepted in all authenticity by the individuals who compose it. The intellectual context in which modern democratic theory first began to be elaborated was one of very varying degrees of moral ambition. The most morally demanding strands of political theory which descend from Rousseau to the present day have certainly not lessened in immediate political charm since the 1760s. But they *have* lost greatly in intellectual plausibility. Both Marx[49] and, under somewhat different inspiration, Adolf Hitler[50] saw an intimate link between Communism and democracy. But to discern any such intimate tie today, whichever way the direction of causality is presumed to run, requires the eye of faith.

Democratic theory in this strong sense, the theory of a community life in which men could live together without one holding power over another, a community whose service is perfect freedom, from which the very fact of power to harm has passed away, has become once again an abstract moral standard and ceased to be any longer a reasoned theoretical expectation about the human future. It continues to feature prominently enough in international speech as a mode of

Frederick Engels, *Collected Works*, Vol. 6, London 1976, esp. pp. 487–506. Also *The German Ideology* (1845–46), *Collected Works*, Vol. 5, London 1976, esp. pp. 48–54; and the *Economic and Philosophical Manuscripts* (1844), *Collected Works*, Vol. 3, London 1975, esp. pp. 296–7.

49 For a well-documented, if somewhat over-argued, presentation of the essentially democratic character of Marx's political theory see Richard N. Hunt, *The Political Ideas of Marx and Engels*, Vol. I, 'Marxism and Totalitarian Democracy 1818–1850', London 1975. For a broader treatment which reaches similar conclusions see Hal Draper, *Karl Marx's Theory of Revolution, Part I: State and Bureaucracy*, 2 vols. New York 1977.

50 For Hitler democracy was quite literally the unacceptable aspect of Marxism: 'National Socialism is what Marxism could have been had it freed itself from the absurd, artificial link with a democratic system' (quoted from Joachim C. Fest, *Hitler*, pb. ed. Harmondsworth 1977, p. 188). See especially Hitler's speech to the Düsseldorf Industry Club on 26 January 1932, Fest, *op. cit.*, p. 459: esp. 'In the economic sphere communism is analogous to democracy in the political sphere' and his characterization of the Nazi party in the same speech as 'the sole party in whose adherents not only the conception of internationalism but also the idea of democracy has been completely overcome, which in its entire organization acknowledges the principles of Command and Obedience', *op. cit.*, p. 461.

ritualized disingenuousness. But perhaps only students in liberal capitalist countries still believe it to have anything to do with political reality.

But the weaker versions of democratic theory prevalent in capitalist societies, being so much less demanding, have been less thoroughly chastened by exposure to historical experience. They have, of course, changed in some respects since their original formulations in the late eighteenth century. It would not be easy, except perhaps among economists, to find modern writers on democracy who assume, as Tom Paine[51] or the Abbé Sieyès[52] did in 1789 or Bentham[53] and James Mill[54] explicitly claimed somewhat later, that there were no real con-

51 Thomas Paine, *The Rights of Man*, Part II (1792), London 1915, pp. 214–19, 230, 259, 265.
52 Sieyès, *Third Estate*, pp. 53–4, 77–8, 184–5 and especially 162–3 (the law 'does not prevent anyone, according to his natural or acquired capacities, according to more or less favourable accidents, from increasing his property with all that a prosperous fortune or a more productive labour can add to it, nor from being able, without *expanding beyond* his legal position, to rise or to create for himself the type of happiness most suited to his taste and most worthy of envy. The law, by protecting the common rights of every citizen, protects each citizen in all that he can become up to the point when his efforts tend to prove harmful to the rights of others.' And for a magnificently complete misjudgement of the disruptive potential of the idea of *égalité* see the note added by Sieyès, *op. cit.*, pp. 198–9).
53 There has been considerable dispute over the question of how far Bentham can be accurately described as a laissez-faire economist and as to whether he believed that a natural harmony of interests was necessarily generated by the individual pursuit of egoistically conceived advantage. Thus formulated, neither of these claims is persuasive. Bentham clearly approved of some governmental interventions in the market; and the central role of the Legislator within his theory would have been otiose if he had believed that individual egoism necessarily generated collective advantage. On Bentham's economics see *Jeremy Bentham's Economic Writings*, ed. Werner Stark, 3 vols., London 1952–54. For the purported natural identification of interests see Elie Halévy, *The Growth of Philosophic Radicalism*, tr. M. Morris, London 1928, p. 15 etc., David Lyons, *In the Interest of the Governed: A Study in Bentham's Philosophy of Law*, Oxford 1973, pp. 11–105. James Steintrager, *Bentham*, pb. ed. London 1977 offers a sensible corrective. Bentham's conviction of the absence of conflict of interest intrinsic to capitalist society as such (and thus beyond the control of good governors) is best shown by his intellectual conversion to democracy in old age and by the character of the reasoning on which this was based (see e.g. Steintrager, *op. cit.*, p. 105).
54 See James Mill, *An Essay on Government* (1819), pb. ed. New York 1955. For the implicit contradictions within Mill's view cf. p. 84 with pp. 90–1. There is an interesting discussion of the rationale of Mill's position in William Thomas, 'James Mill's Politics: The *Essay on Government* and the Movement for Reform, *The Historical Journal*, XII, 2, June 1969, pp. 249–84. See also the subsequent controversy with Wendell R. Carr, *Historical Journal*, XIV, 3, September 1971, 553–80; Vol. XIV, 4, December 1971, 735–50; Vol. XV, 2, June 1972, 315–20. One modern philosopher who makes a bold effort to sustain the assumption is Robert Nozick, *Anarchy, State and Utopia*, Oxford 1974.

flicts of economic and political interest intrinsic to capitalist society. But there are still ample exponents of the view that capitalist democracy is not merely the only democracy we yet have – but also the best democracy we are ever likely to have, let alone to be able to retain for any length of time. Capitalist democratic theory (as we may provisionally call it) accepts, as it always has accepted, states more or less as it finds them. It accepts that government is necessary, expedient, and presumes that it will always remain so. Although it has no very explicit affection for governmental power, it also has no very fastidious revulsion from it, presuming that if it is indeed expedient, it can hardly *seriously* be judged to be an evil.

Modern states, to be sure, are far more intensely ruled than the states of early nineteenth century Europe and the sense of the range of potential political hazards against which it may be expedient to guard has widened appreciably since James Mill. But it remains broadly true that capitalist democratic theory accepts capitalist democracies as it finds them, very much *faute de mieux*, as imperfect devices for fending off worse fates. We can look at this modest trajectory of accommodation, conveniently, by setting the arguments of James Mill's *Essay on Government* against more modern versions of the same line of thought, such as those of the émigré Austrian economist Joseph Schumpeter or the pluralist theories of contemporary American writers like Robert Dahl and Seymour Martin Lipset. James Mill saw government simply as a mechanism for restraining the misbehaviour of essentially and limitlessly selfish men.[55] There was simply no limit to how badly any human being could be expected to behave, if only they could get away with it. In evidence for this gloomy claim he produced the conduct of British slave-owners in the West Indies,[56] a distressingly apt example. Government was necessary, then, truly indispensable indeed, because all human beings were axiomatically untrustworthy. If men were to be safe at all in each other's company, they needed a fundamentally external guarantee of their security – a familiar Hobbesian argument. But one which, as in the case of Hobbe's *Leviathan* itself, posed further problems of its own of some severity. As John Locke expressed the key objection to it:

55 James Mill, *op. cit.*, pp. 55–60 esp. p. 59 ('Terror is the grand instrument').
56 James Mill, *op. cit.*, pp. 60–1, esp. 61 ('It is proved, therefore, by the closest deduction from the acknowledged laws of human nature, and by direct and decisive experiments, that the ruling *one* or the ruling *few* would, if checks did not operate in the way of prevention, reduce the great mass of the people subject to their power at least to the condition of Negroes in the West Indies').

'This is to think that Men are so foolish that they take care to avoid what Mischiefs may be done them by *Pole-cats* or *Foxes*, but are content, nay think it Safety, to be devoured by *Lions*.'[57]

If all men were fundamentally untrustworthy and if only subjection to government could render them trustworthy, then what precisely could render the government itself trustworthy? Mill's answer to his problem, stated in these stark terms, is not impressive. It operates essentially in two stages, restricting the main hazard of malign power briskly in the first stage to that of theft[58] (an imaginatively more constricted sense of risk than the example of the West Indian slave owners suggests) – and, in the second stage, proposing that the representative governors should be elected to serve only for very *short* periods of time.[59] Under these conditions, Mill reasoned, they would not be able to steal enough during their term of office to compensate themselves for the social costs of their poor stewardship when they duly returned to private life. Having disposed somewhat optimistically in this way of an alarming hiatus at the centre of his theory, Mill confined himself for most of the rest of his *Essay* to arguing for a broad franchise in order to remove any motive for the voters as an independent group to exploit the rest of the population. In this section he relaxed the rigorous assumption of mutual human antipathy to some extent – not claiming that universal adult suffrage was undesirable but insisting, in the light of the fact that it was politically highly unpopular as a prospect among those who already held votes, that it probably would not make much difference if children, women and men under middle age and possibly the very poor were excluded from the franchise, since the interests of all of them were included in those of the residual group.[60] Finally, confronting the prospect that the poorer would use political power to expropriate the rich, he abandoned his psychological assumptions completely and argued instead that there was no risk of the poor threatening the existing institutions of private property (so unlike the political climate of ancient Greece with its incessant warcry for the abolition of debts and redistribution of land)

---

57 John Locke, *Two Treatises of Government*, ed. P. Laslett, 2nd ed. Cambridge 1967, II, para. 93, ll. 30–2, p. 346. As Laslett points out (p. 346n), there is no reason to assume that the target of Locke's argument at this point was in fact Hobbes himself. What is important here is simply that Locke's objection constitutes a strong reason for rejecting Hobbe's line of thought.
58 James Mill, *op. cit.*, pp. 49–50.
59 James Mill, *op. cit.*, pp. 69–72.
60 James Mill, *op. cit.*, pp. 73–7. For discussion of the context of Mill's franchise proposals see the articles cited in note 54 above.

because the poor in Britain were then (and could always be trusted to remain) under the ideological hegemony of the middle classes.[61] Mill was not exactly a subtle political observer or sociologist. But in this respect, the respect least integrated into his formal political theory, his intuitions were for a good century and a half closer to the actual line of development of capitalist democracy than Marx's later assumption of a clear functional incompatibility over time between democratic politics and capitalist society.

Mill's theory, if one disregards its vagaries, was a simple theory of rational individual choice. It had virtually no distinct institutional component at all. It was a psychological, not a sociological theory. The more prominent modern versions of capitalist democratic theory are on the whole sociologically less spare. Joseph Schumpeter, for example, argued in his *Capitalism, Socialism and Democracy* that an account of modern democratic politics in terms of the rational individual choices of citizens was wilfully obscurantist; and he presented instead an alternative model in which professional politicians grouped in organized political parties which function like firms on a market compete for the allegiance of voters at lengthy intervals and the successful competitors rule the state (with rather little distraction) in the intervening periods. Democracies are distinguished from non-democracies by the way in which they acquire their rulers, not by the sorts of power which the rulers hold whilst they are rulers.[62] A second modification of capitalist democratic theory, predominantly American in provenance, though drawing its roots in part from de Tocqueville, emphasizes not simply the formal mechanism whereby rulers are selected but – in contrast with the political arrangements of Communist or above all of Fascist states – the freedom of a multiplicity of groups to associate to further their political interests.[63] Robert Dahl, for example, described the United States as displaying a pluralism of all

61 James Mill, *op. cit.*, pp. 90–1.
62 Joseph Schumpeter, *Capitalism, Socialism and Democracy*, London 1943, esp. cap. XXII.
63 There is as yet no very illuminating intellectual history of the development of this current of thought and feeling and it has been identified as a distinct ideological movement largely by those who have rejected it. Its leading figures included Daniel Bell, Seymour Martin Lipset, Robert Dahl, William Kornhauser, David Truman and from some points of view the sociologist Talcott Parsons. For a sample of the critics see Henry S. Kariel, *The Decline of American Pluralism*, Stanford, Calif. 1961; Robert Paul Wolff, 'Beyond Tolerance' in R. P. Wolff, Barrington Moore & Herbert Marcuse, *A Critique of Pure Tolerance*, Boston 1965; R. P. Wolff, *The Poverty of Liberalism* pb. ed. Boston 1969; Steven Lukes, *Power: A Radical View*, pb. ed. London 1974; Alvin Gouldner, *The Coming Crisis of Western Sociology*, pb. ed. London 1971.

active and legitimate groups.[64] And other pluralists like Lipset accepted with equal cheerfulness a mass of evidence that the American political order favoured the wealthy and well organized against the poor and disorganized for all it and they were worth, that it came, indeed, very close to being an unusually broad oligarchy (a broader oligarchy, of course, than the 'democracy' of ancient Athens). Any grouping which could organize actively could enter into American politics; and if it turned out that the working class and above all the poorer ethnic minorities were distinctly less able to get themselves actively organized than, for example, large-scale farmers or Texas oil-well owners, then that was no great cost because the working class and the poorer ethnic minorites were, it turned out, decidedly more ambivalent in the attitudes which they expressed towards the values of American democracy than those who were doing more handsomely out of it.[65] America was the stablest of all democracies and the most pluralist of all democracies; and, if it turned out that it was also less *politically* egalitarian than had previously been suspected or at least claimed, then *this* meant that the findings of American political science (a notoriously value free intellectual practice) were that stable and authentically pluralist democracy was somewhat more oligarchical than had previously been supposed (or, at least, acknowledged).[66] Even in its own dreary terms the democratic government offered in this theory seems a somewhat ineffective mechanism for protecting the interests of quite a number of the governed.

So we have really two distinct and developed democratic theories loose in the world today – one dismally ideological and the other fairly blatantly Utopian. In the first, democracy is the name of a distinct and very palpable form of modern state, at the most optimistic, simply the least bad mechanism for securing some measure of responsibility of the governors to the governed within modern states.[67] In the second,

---

64 Robert A. Dahl, *A Preface to Democratic Theory*, pb. ed. Chicago 1956, esp. p. 137. For the further development of Dahl's views on pluralist regimes, the possible extent of political participation in modern societies and the degree to which substantive pluralism depends upon capitalism see Robert A. Dahl, *Who Governs?* pb. ed. New Haven 1961; *After the Revolution?*, pb. ed. New Haven 1970; *Polyarchy: Participation and Opposition*, pb. ed. New Haven 1971; and 'Pluralism Revisited', *Comparative Politics*, X, 2, January 1978, pp. 191–203.
65 See especially Seymour M. Lipset, *Political Man*, London 1960.
66 An economical presentation of this drift of thought can be found in Quentin Skinner, 'The Empirical Theorists of Democracy: A Plague on Both Their Houses', *Political Theory*, I, 3, August 1973, pp. 287–306.
67 It is the great merit of Plamenatz's otherwise oversanguine text (J. P. Plamenatz,

democracy (or as it is sometimes called participatory democracy)[68] is close to meaning simply the good society in operation, a society in which we produce as profusely as we do today, if less wastefully and with better taste – and in which all social arrangements authentically represent the interests of all persons, in which all live actively in and for their society and yet all remain as free as before (where *before* means roughly as they could urgently and excusably desire).

We shall not readily lose the modern state; and we have really no good reason to suppose that the human race as a whole will survive its passing, if we do do so. So we do *need* a theory of how the governments of modern states can least badly be controlled. But neither shall we readily lose the fiercely demanding images of human fulfilment and human liberty which indict the reality of *every* modern state and modern society. To exist, as we are now compelled to do, at the intersection of these incompatible rationalities is to be sentenced politically to a condition of ineradicable bad faith.

If we are all democrats today, it is not a very cheerful fate to share. Today, in politics, democracy is the *name* for what we cannot have[69] – yet cannot cease to want.

Democracy and Illusion, London 1973) to have insisted so bluntly that it is scarcely possible to overestimate the importance of this project.

68 For a clear, if somewhat innocent, exposition of the merits of participatory democracy see Carole Pateman, *Participation and Democratic Theory*, Cambridge 1970.

69 The possibility which we are denied is the possibility of *ruling* our own state. We are not, of course, as recent American history shows, deprived of the possibility through a variety of forms of action, legal or otherwise, of entrenching on the possibilities for others to misrule it or to commit it to reprehensible political ventures abroad for lengthy periods of time. Still less are we precluded from democratizing the exercise of power below the state level. In most (if not all) subordinate institutions of modern society, capitalist or otherwise, the opportunities for democratization of an unequivocally beneficial kind remain all too abundant. (In many contexts they also remain opportunities which are extremely difficult to take up.) A democratic organization of an institution is not one which elides the authority of skill, knowledge and understanding but simply one in which such authority is compelled persistently to demonstrate its force to those concerned in terms which they can grasp and, by dint of being so compelled, is made in some real measure responsible to them. Such arrangements are not always either agreeable for the authoritative or economical in the use which they make of people's time.

vvv

Liberalism

'Don't, I beseech you, *generalize* too much in these sympathies and tender-
nesses – remember that every life is a special problem which is not yours but
another's and content yourself with the terrible algebra of your own.'
     Henry James, letter to Grace Norton 1883 (quoted from Leon Edel,
Henry James: The Conquest of London, London 1962, p. 505).

Liberalism is a much less neatly bounded topic than democratic
theory; and, in consequence, it is a much harder topic to discuss with
any great clarity. Considering democratic theory, it is natural to focus
at first on a central paradox – that we have all become democrats in
theory at just that stage of history at which it has become virtually
impossible for us in practice to organize our social life in a democratic
fashion any longer. It may not be open to us to resolve this paradox; but
at least it can serve – as Dr Johnson observed of the prospect of being
hanged in a fortnight,[1] to concentrate our minds wonderfully. But, in
the case of liberalism by contrast, it is by no means obvious what there
is for us to concentrate our minds upon. Even its most savage critics (at
least if one excepts Nietzsche)[2] are fundamentally undecided as to
whether they have come to destroy liberalism or to fulfil it – as to
whether what liberalism offers is an improperly fussy criterion for the
organization of human collective life or a genuine project of human
liberation which simply *happens* to be inadequate in the mechanisms
which it suggests for reaching this goal. In politics, this ambivalence is
quite important because it constitutes an indecision between the view

1 James Boswell, *The Life of Samuel Johnson LLD*, London 1906, Vol. 2, p. 123.
2 Nietzsche's critique of liberalism is scattered throughout his writings. For a helpful
  introduction see J. P. Stern, *Nietzsche*, pb. ed. London 1978. For perhaps the most
  illuminating single text see Friedrich Nietzsche, *Beyond Good and Evil*, tr. R. Hollingdale, pb. ed. Harmondsworth 1973; and for an interesting selection of passages from
  the full range of his writings see R. J. Hollingdale (ed.), *A Nietzsche Reader*, pb. ed.
  Harmondsworth 1977, esp. pp. 71–124, 149–66, 197–205.

that liberals are morally vicious and the less inflammatory view that they are simply sociologically naive.

A second major difficulty with the analysis of liberalism lies in the term's extreme imprecision of reference. We may for a variety of motives, good, bad and indifferent, disagree on what constitute the necessary and sufficient conditions for being a democrat. But at least no one is likely to dispute that being a democrat is a fundamentally *political* value. In the case of liberalism, however, matters are very much less clear. In self-description at any rate, being a liberal is often a matter of broad cultural allegiance and not of politics at all – or certainly not of the major organizational issues of politics. If the central dispositional value of liberals is tolerance, their central *political* value is perhaps a fundamental antipathy towards authority in any of its forms. The antithesis of liberalism is certainly not socialism – however much laissez-faire economists like Friedman[3] or Hayek may wish to persuade us that it is so. It is perhaps closer to a helpful starting point to suggest two different antitheses for liberalism – antitheses which give to the word liberalism itself slightly different senses: firstly conservatism and secondly autocracy.

Dispositionally, liberalism has little regard for the past. It certainly refuses wholly to see the past as an authoritative focus of value. Liberals suspect tradition; and they were, at least for a time, very ready to believe in the reality of progress. In the *Querelle*[4] between the Ancients and the Moderns in the seventeenth century, Liberals stood firmly with the Moderns. They stood wholly with the Moderns in substance, of course, because at that point in time modernity stood pretty firmly with them. But as time went by modernity turned out to be a somewhat treacherous ally. The watershed essentially was the French Revolution, a revolution made in the name of Liberal values – Liberty, Equality, Reason – and one made against tradition and against

3 Both Friedman and Hayek have written prolifically. For the gist of their identifications of liberalism and socialism see Milton Friedman (& Rose D. Friedman), *Capitalism and Freedom*, pb. ed. Chicago 1963; and F. A. Hayek, *New Studies in Philosophy, Politics, Economics and the History of Ideas*, London 1978, pp. 3–162, 179–90.

4 For details of the *Querelle* see J. B. Bury, *The Idea of Progress*, pb. ed. New York 1955, caps. IV–VI: John Passmore, *The Perfectibility of Man*, pb. ed. London 1972, cap. X; J. S. Spink, *French Free Thought from Gassendi to Voltaire*, London 1960; Richard F. Jones, *Ancients and Moderns: A Study of the Rise of the Scientific Movement in Seventeenth-century England*, 2nd ed. St Louis, Missouri 1961; Paul Hazard, *La Crise de la conscience européenne 1680–1715*, Paris 1961; and for one of the classic texts see Bernard le Bovier de Fontenelle, *Digression sur les anciens et les modernes*, edited with *Entretiens sur la pluralité des mondes*, by Robert Shackleton, Oxford 1955.

arbitrary privilege. But also, to be sure, a revolution which culminated in blood and terror and which in due course ended in a military autocracy. After 1793 and the Jacobin dictatorship of the Committee of Public Safety under Robespierre liberals no longer found it so easy to trust the future and to regard conservative values as unmitigatedly in error. Seeing their revolutionary opponents as having misconceived the meaning of the liberal values of liberty and reason and misunderstood the fundamental characteristics of human nature – and seeing revolutionary autocracy as both a fundamental denial of liberal values *and* a logical outcome of the revolutionary misinterpretation of the demands of liberty and reason, Liberals began to see more merit in tradition and in the past. In his *Memoirs* Alexis de Tocqueville described his own political mission during the 1848 revolution in France, as any good Liberal might have done, as defending the cause of 'liberty and the dignity of mankind'; but he also described himself, in a phrase which even Burke would have been happy to sanction, as seeking 'to protect the ancient laws of Society against the innovators'.[5] In the eighteenth century a liberal like Voltaire could summarize his political and cultural objectives with little hesitation in the terse slogan '*Écrasez l' infâme*'.[6] But the minds of modern liberals are haunted by the grim understanding that an over-vigorous attempt to dispose of infamy can readily result in the gratuitous destruction of much else besides: that even if it is not possible to make omelettes without breaking eggs, it is child's play to break eggs by the dozen, without contriving to make any kind of an omelette at all.

But if liberals can no longer blindly trust the future, if they can no longer believe in a guaranteed progress, what precisely *can* they believe in? It is, after all, scarcely a criticism of their intellectual honesty or skill that they *can* no longer trust the future so absolutely. Today we may still hope to avoid regress. We may strive as best we can to improve those parts of the world which lie within our own grasp. But who now, except a complete imbecile, can still *expect* a *guaranteed* progress? In the eighteenth or nineteenth or even the early twentieth

---

5 Alexis de Tocqueville, *Recollections*, tr. A. Texeira de Mattos, pb. ed. New York 1959, p. 116 ('with the help,' he continues, 'of the new force which the republican principle might lend to the government; to cause the evident will of the French people to triumph over the passions and desires of the Paris workmen; to conquer demagogism with democracy'. While there is evident room for dispute about the terms in which it is described, it must be noted that this was a program with a future).

6 On Voltaire's politics see the admirable study by Peter Gay, *Voltaire's Politics: The Poet as Realist*, Princeton, N.J. 1959; and especially (for the centrality of this slogan) see pp. 239–72.

centuries – before the First World War began – liberals could still trust in the progressive dynamic of history because history (as seen from western Europe at least) was in essence the unfolding of reason, the cultural passage from superstition to rational comprehension, and – its political analogue – the passage from subjection to individual autonomy. Today such a vision of cultural transformation, even for those who can sustain their cultural conviction, looks politically and militarily exposed to a degree. Hegel, in the early nineteenth century, saw the immanent progress in history, working its way out through the projects of men, with other lesser matters on their minds; and christened it appreciatively 'the Cunning of Reason'.[7] Today, we are on the whole more impressed by the Cunning of Unreason. It is hard any longer to see History as going Reason's way.

But if liberals are more despondent today than they were in 1900 or 1789, they are not necessarily any less trusting in reason itself. They know, of course, being well educated and sophisticated persons, that reasoning can take the form of rationalization, the finding of ingenious reasons for conclusions already adopted more or less compulsively. They read Marx and Freud and know that much which sounds reasonable does so because it articulates the structural requirements of social credulity or the individual subconscious. But they also know that Marx and Freud were good rationalists like themselves and that Marxist or Freudian explanations, if they are coherent and valid, are in themselves nothing more nor less than conclusions of human reason. Initially, political rationalism, the view that politics can and should be shaped by rational understanding, was simply a weapon against conservatism, a method of rejecting political claims based simply on tradition or supposedly sacred authority. In a political culture in which almost all legal and political arguments were based upon claims about the past, the political appeal to reason was explicitly revolutionary, a sudden escape from history. The Leveller, Richard Overton put it well in his address to Parliament in 1646:[8] 'yee were chosen to worke our deliverance, and to Estate us in naturall and just libertie agreeable to

7 For this conception see Georg Wilhelm Friedrich Hegel, *Lectures on the Philosophy of World History: Introduction: Reason in History*, tr. H. B. Nisbet, Cambridge 1975, esp. pp. 79–89 (the famous phrase 'the cunning of reason' appears on p. 89). For contrasting treatments of Hegel's conception of historical process see the introduction to *Lectures* by Duncan Forbes; Charles Taylor, *Hegel*, Cambridge 1975; Shlomo Avineri, *Hegel's Theory of the Modern State*, Cambridge 1972.

8 (Richard Overton), *A Remonstrance of Many Thousand Citizens and other Free-born People of England* . . . (in William Haller (ed.), *Tracts on Liberty in the Puritan Revolution, 1638–1647*, New York 1934, Vol. 3, pp. 354–5).

Reason and common *equitie*; for whatever our Fore-fathers were; or whatever they did or suffered, or were enforced to yeeld unto; we are the men of the present age, and ought to be absolutely free from all kindes of exorbitancies, molestations or *Arbitrary Power'*. Today liberals know only too well that working our political deliverance is no simple task. But they have scarcely come by any more *promising* criterion for determining their political commitments than Overton's 'reason and common equity'; and, those who still see themselves as liberals today are likely to feel that they neither have been given, nor could in principle have been given, a sound motive for abandoning it.

We have already mustered a dismaying number of categories for setting out the main features of liberalism: political rationalism, hostility to autocracy, cultural distaste for conservatism and for tradition in general, tolerance. But there is one further category which we need to note explicitly before we can begin a historical account of liberalism's development and fate. This category is in some ways the most elusive of the lot. Indeed it is not even clear what is the right verbal form under which to consider it. Liberalism, it is sometimes said, is a form of *individualism*.[9] Liberal thinkers seek to understand society, state and economy as the sum of the actions of individuals. Indeed they have even developed a systematic professional intellectual ideology for this practice, known as *methodological individualism*,[10] which insists that this is the only non-superstitious way in which these entities *can* be understood, that there is literally nothing else *there* to understand but one damned individual after another. In their politics liberals defend tenaciously the rights of individuals; and at least in their overt cultural preferences they set great store by, they cherish, the development of individuality. These dimensions of commitment to the individual are extremely various, straying between biological and sociological and moral and cultural judgements. They do not necessarily *fit* at all well together. The evaluative flavour of current English speech is plainly more sympathetic to some of them than it is to others. As a purely cultural value, it secures, at least in cultivated circles, a fairly strong allegiance. To be individual is to be distinctive – an accomplishment or perhaps a happy biological accident. To be the reverse of individual is to be nondescript. Schoolchildren, for example, are often extremely anxious to be nondescript, not to stand out. But among cultivated

9 For an interesting and brief overall conspectus of this tradition of thought and feeling see Steven Lukes, *Individualism*, Oxford 1973.
10 See John O'Neill (ed.), *Modes of Individualism and Collectivism*, London 1973.

adults, to be individual is to stand out felicitously, a less ambivalent judgement, for example, than to be eccentric. It is, in short, to be well on the way towards being enviable. What cultivated person would not prefer being individual to being nondescript?

Now emphasizing the socially specific setting of these values does bring out at least one way in which their favourable tone *can* be reversed. The cultivated middle class's regard for individuality is not merely a regard which distinguishes it pretty sharply from the unculti- vated middle classes, hinting at a cultural heritage from Romanticism and a certain social broadening in the appeals of the *vie de bohème*. It also distinguishes it at least equally sharply from the working classes. Individuality is not an explicitly proletarian *value*. And the political apparatuses which seek officially to represent the values of the pro- letariat (whatever one may think of the authenticity and proficiency of their efforts to do so) have characteristically shown a rather developed hostility to individuality as a cultural value. A Hundred Flowers have Bloomed briefly; and in the Soviet Union in the immediate aftermath of the revolution many bold experiments were essayed. But, in the longer run, political liberalism and the protection of cultural individuality have looked reasonably natural companions, while state socialism has looked an altogether more austere cultural patron.

To be individual is to be distinctive. But to be *an* individual is not distinctive at all – merely the human condition – a fate from which even the direct prophets of mass society are unlikely to foresee our rescue. That we *are* all individuals is a palpable biological fact; but hardly one which bears in itself any obvious political or cultural or moral signifi- cance. It is hard to conceive of a perspective from which the *fact* could be intelligibly denied; and if this was all that methodological indi- vidualists were committed to, it is hard to see how they could muster any opponents.

To be individual, then, is to be distinctive; and to be an individual is simply the common human fate. But to be an individual*ist* is to embrace this fate with a suspicious alacrity, to make a vice out of necessity. Being individual – in aspiration at least – is simply doing one's own thing, a private concern or a consensual pleasure. But being an individual*ist* is well on the way towards disregarding the interests of others or denying the presence of any basic affective commitment of one human being towards another. Being individual is an almost purely aesthetic category and on the whole an affirmative one. Being an individualist is plainly a moral category and veering strongly towards a negative one. Speaking in caricature one may say that there are two main varieties of liberalism and that they have, each, a distinctive psychology to go with them. One is rationalist and inclined towards transcendence, much preoccupied with the aesthetics of consciousness. The other is mechanical and reductive, with a strong propensity to reduce human nature to a stream of intrinsically meaningless and self-referential desires. The politics of these two strands have both varied very widely. But one can say broadly that the first – the rationalist, the transcendent and the aesthetic was the liberalism that Marxism (following Hegel) saw itself as coming to fulfil, while the second, despite Marx's dogged insistence on the primacy of the economic, was the liberalism which he came to bury. There is no doubt that the second has a sharper intellectual profile and a clearer historical pedigree. It is a creature of the triumph of capitalism and of the mechanization of the world picture which accompanied the scientific revolution of the seventeenth century.[11] This is a liberalism whose political

11 The most striking portrait of the unity of the process of intellectual, economic and political development from which modern European society emerges remains that given by the youthful Georg Lukács in *History and Class Consciousness* (1923), tr. R. Livingstone, London 1971. Scholars have not as yet succeeded (and may well indeed never suceed) in distinguishing clearly and assessing convincingly the precise lines of causality within this intricate development. Nor can it be said at present that the development of natural science or liberal political and moral thought or capitalist production or modern state forms have been very convincingly treated separately. What is intended here is simply the claim that these forms of thought and practice have evolved over the same timespan and that it is still an open question (which in the case of Lukács has been pressed even in the case of natural science) how far the cultural products are even in principle viable without the shelter of the distinctive rationality of the social, economic and political forms which have accompanied their emergence. (To note that one process is causally related to another does not imply the absurd claim that what can be truly asserted about the former necessarily in itself constitutes in any sense the explanation (or even *an* explanation) of the latter.) For a variety of conceptions (some strikingly more convincing than others) of the relations or disjunctions between different components of this process of rationalization see: Edwin A. Burtt, *The Metaphysical Foundations of Modern Physical Science*, pb. ed. Garden City, N. Y. 1954; Edward J. Dijksterhuis, *The Mechanization of the World Picture*, tr. C. Dikshoorn, Oxford 1961; Alexander Koyré, *From the Closed World to the Infinite Universe*, pb. ed. New York 1958; Charles Webster, *The Great Instauration: Science, Medicine and Reform 1626–1660*, London 1975; William Leiss, *The Domination of Nature*, New York 1972; Roy S. Porter, *The Making of Geology: Earth Science in Britain 1660–1815*, Cambridge 1977; C. B. Macpherson, *The Political Theory of Possessive Individualism*, Oxford 1962. Even the finest presentations of the process in its more socially extended forms find it difficult to transcend the picture of the dawn of the evident (our own rationality) largely under its own weight: see especially Keith Thomas's superlative *Religion and the Decline of Magic: Studies in Popular Beliefs in Sixteenth- and Seventeenth-Century England*, pb. ed. Harmondsworth 1973 and 'An Anthropology of Religion and Magic II', *Journal of Inter-disciplinary History*, VI, 1,

properties have been adequately explored since the eighteenth century; and both its merits and its disfigurements are plain enough. It is the liberalism of the pluralist democracies of the western world, the states which permit their intellectuals the licence to exercise their wits and their imaginations in public on the meaning of political existence. The historical domain of this brand of liberalism has been confined to Europe (and largely to western Europe at that) and to the European diaspora in North America and the Antipodes. Its fate is bound up with the fate of the capitalist mode of production, an economic invention which came very close to conquering the globe, which may now be beginning to ebb, but which has hardly yet been surpassed as a productive system in its heartlands (as Marx for example expected) by the creation of any *more* effective productive system to replace it. Liberalism, in this sense, is simply the political form (or perhaps one should say the acceptable political form) of capitalist production, a form which has changed, as capitalist production itself has changed, though not necessarily in any very intimate harmony or resonance with the changes in the latter.

The future of capitalism is not a suitable topic on which to dogmatize. In this case it is simply foolhardy to offer *any* assurances about the future. In 1848 Marx and Engels were exceedingly confident that capitalism in France and England could not last long[12] and in 1965 (if the diminuendo can be pardoned) Andrew Shonfield was also fairly

Summer 1975, 91–109 and cf. Jeanne Favret-Saada, *Les Mots, la mort, les sorts; la sorcellerie dans le Bocage*, Paris 1977. For two stimulating attempts to analyse the relations between economic and social organization and the development of state forms in Europe in the course of the (protracted) transition from feudalism to capitalism see Immanuel Wallerstein, *The Modern World System*, pb. ed. London 1974 and especially Perry Anderson, *Passages from Antiquity to Feudalism*, and *Lineages of the Absolutist State*, London 1974. And for searching criticism of each author see the reviews by Theda Skocpol, *American Journal of Sociology*, LXXXII, March 1977, 1075–90; and (with Mary Fulbrook), *Journal of Development Studies*, XIII, 3, April 1977, 290–5. See also Peter Gourevitch, 'The International System and Regime Formation', *Comparative Politics*, X, 3, April 1978, 419–38.

12 See *Manifesto of the Communist Party*, Marx & Engels, *Collected Works*, Vol. 6, London 1976. In the aftermath of the failures of 1848–50, their sense of imminence weakened: see e.g. *Minutes of the Central Committee Meeting of the Communist League*, 15 Sept. 1850 (Karl Marx, *The Revolutions of 1848*, ed. D. Fernbach, pb. ed. Harmondsworth 1973, p. 341). But this did not diminish their confidence in the eventual realization of the conceptions set out in the *Manifesto*: see e.g. *The Class Struggles in France 1848 to 1850*, Karl Marx, *Surveys from Exile*, ed. D. Fernbach, pb. ed. Harmondsworth 1973, p. 131: 'A new revolution is only possible as a result of a new crisis; but it will come, just as surely as the crisis itself.' and the Review of Guizot's book on the English Revolution, *Surveys from Exile*, p. 225 etc.

certain that modern capitalism had learnt how to run itself more or less indefinitely.[13] Little enduring ground is apparent for the confidence of either party and no way at all has yet been presented in which one could *know* which is going to be proved right or rather proved least wrong in another fifty years or so. This obscurity is quite important in its implications for how one judges this brand of liberalism politically, whether or not one's own politics are plausibly described as liberal in the round. If the civil liberties and substantive pluralism of capitalist democracies are thoroughly established, if notably untranscendent, goods, it may be proper to take a fairly sardonic line about these, indicating tartly, historically speaking where they got on and morally speaking where they get off. But if they are wholly historically contingent, in no way *guaranteed*, embellishments of the human political future, then the terms of trade between cultural fastidiousness and political commitment ought perhaps to shift rather sharply and the culturally exigent come to adopt a more modest tone. In a confidently Marxist mood, it would be natural to seek to display the relation between these two liberalisms as one of stark and fundamental antipathy, a war to the death; and then, certainly, it would not be difficult to choose which side to pick – generosity and creativity (the virtues of the aristocrat and the artist) against greed and cowardice (the vices of the peasant and the bourgeois). But in a despondent and anti-Marxist mood, the relations might look rather different; and the fine cult of individuality, the respect for the efflorescence of human personality and creativity might come to look politically very *crudely* dependent on the modest politics of the bourgeoisie; and the same cult of individuality, if turned into a self-subsistent politics of its own (as perhaps in certain kinds of anarchism) might come to seem a tasteless exercise in vanity and self-deception, a bland denial of the realities of blood and pain and need and danger which the drabber liberal ideology of capitalist reproduction has never (to its credit) forgotten. In practice there seem sound reasons for shifting between the two viewpoints, since neither can make any plausible pretence to comprehensive validity.

We may begin with the late seventeenth century English philosopher, John Locke, the most celebrated exponent of the value of tolerance, the leading apologist of liberal constitutionalism in political theory – at a time when liberal constitutionalism was still an ideologi-

13 Andrew Shonfield, *Modern Capitalism: The Changing Balance of Public and Private Power*, London 1965.

cally subversive conception[14] – the first, too, of the great British empiricist philosophers and a stalwart exponent of the claims of reason in human life. Add to these attributes, as Marxist scholars have hastened to do,[15] that Locke was incautious enough to describe the purpose of government as the preservation of property, that he derives all social obligations from the rationally conceived obligations of individuals and that he had a fundamentally egoistic (that is to say – selfish) theory of human motivation and it is easy to see Locke as the conclusive vindication of the Marxist judgement on reductive liberalism, its origins and its gross moral disfigurements. Taken together, Locke's three major works, the *Letter on Toleration*, the *Two Treatises of Government*, and the great *Essay concerning Human Understanding*, give at first glance a comprehensive philosophy unequalled in range and force and the integrity of its liberal commitment until the works of John Stuart Mill. The negative judgement of liberalism (that of Professor Macpherson, for example) would see the transition from Locke to John Stuart Mill as a move from the callow assurance of early capitalist society to a more sophisticated and sensitive unease, a dawning awareness of the grave moral limitations inherent in capitalist society, its narrow vision, its sordid instrumentalism and its corrupting social psychology. Locke, coming early in the history of capitalist ideology, could see only the massive enhancement of human freedom which these institutions can engender. But Mill, coming later, was able to sense more clearly the heavy cost to human capacities for free self-development which they brought with them. Capitalist society, Mill could see, as Locke could not, fostered a narrow egoist individualism at the expense of free, inventive and generous individuality.[16]

But, in *fact* Locke seems to have had rather different values at heart and rather different goals in mind. If Locke's works represent a comprehensive liberal philosophy at a relatively early stage in the history of liberal ideology (reason, tolerance, government by consent and knowledge, even moral knowlege, based firmly upon sense experience) it is important to ask what exactly *led* Locke to put his trust in these values, what were the cultural and human premises of such an allegiance? Is it in fact the case, as Macpherson for example claims, that Locke puts his

---

14 Just how subversive can be identified clearly from Julian Franklin, *John Locke and the Theory of Sovereignty*, Cambridge 1978.

15 For the most distinguished and scholarly statement of this case see C. B. Macpherson, *Political Theory of Possessive Individualism*, pp. 194–271.

16 Macpherson, *Possessive Individualism*, caps. I & VI and C. B. Macpherson, *Democratic Theory: Essays in Retrieval*, Oxford 1973, caps. I–III.

trust essentially in the moral sufficiency of capitalist market production?[17] Is the property which government is supposed to defend simply and uncritically the private property in economic goods of early capitalist society? The answer, of course, is that it is *not*; that Locke nowhere proclaims a comprehensive moral allegiance to the market and that the property which government is supposed to defend is nothing more nor less than the rights of all men as men in the historical political circumstances in which they find themselves. It is perfectly true that the words property and right are virtually synonymous in Locke's usage. But the term which fixes the synonymy onto our own language is 'right', not 'property'.[18] (That is to say Macpherson's interpretation of this aspect of Locke is simply the systematization of a translation error.)[19] Since the historical circumstances in which Locke found himself were in part (as those in which *we* find ourselves largely remain) those of a capitalist society, it is unsurprising that many of the rights which men held within this society were rights which had come to them through what one might term capitalist channels. But it is simply historically false to presume that Locke allotted to the rights mediated by the market any privileged or over-riding status; and he was entirely ready to see other immediate human needs over-riding them and limiting them.[20] The view that government exists to protect rights is not semantically fashionable among Marxists. But the communist future which Marx envisaged was not a future in which rights were no longer realized. It was a future in which for the first time, as he put it: 'can the narrow horizon of bourgeois right be crossed in its entirety'[21] – a future in which rights would somehow be rendered irrelevant, unnecessary – in which they would be not *negated* but surpassed.

Living when he did and as he did, Locke was by necessity in part a bourgeois political theorist. But insofar as he was a liberal, he was

17 Macpherson, *Possessive Individualism*, pp. 194–262.
18 See the important study of Locke's analysis of property by James Tully (forthcoming, Cambridge University Press 1979).
19 This represents an unusually comprehensive *débâcle* for a homophonic translation theory (see Christopher Hookway, 'Indeterminacy and Interpretation', in C. Hookway & Philip Pettit (eds.), *Action and Interpretation*, Cambridge 1978, pp. 35–6). It should be emphasized that Macpherson himself naturally does not accept that it *is* a mistranslation: *Possessive Individualism*, p. 198.
20 See John Dunn, 'Justice and the Interpretation of Locke's Political Theory', *Political Studies*, XVI, 1, February 1968, pp. 68–87.
21 Karl Marx, *Critique of the Gotha Programme*, Marx & Engels, *Selected Works*, 2 vols., Moscow 1958, Vol. 2, p. 24.

certainly not such *because* of his moral credulity in the market. Nor is there a shred of evidence that any of his major commitments – tolerance, rationality, individual rights and a modest degree of empiricism – had anything directly to do with the specific institutions of capitalism at all. But, if he was not a liberal because he trusted in the market, what precisely was it that he *did* trust in enough to make him treat individual human beings as an equal focus of value and their beliefs as requiring a high degree of tolerance? It cannot, really, after all be said that exposure to capitalist society, life for example for white persons in the Union of South Africa, necessarily commits anyone very deeply to any values vaguely resembling these.

The historical answer is a fairly simple one in essence.[22] What Locke trusted in was the Christian God and his own intelligence; and when it came to the crunch and the two parted company, what he proved to trust in more deeply was the God and not the intelligence.[23] This is self-evidently not a matter for *intellectual* congratulation. But it *is* of great importance for a historical understanding of liberalism. God, the Creator, determined the ends of man, his creature; and all the values which Locke defended were values which he defended as vehicles of God's purposes for man. God gave men reason to understand their situation on earth and, above all, their duty within this situation. He gave them senses as channels through which they could apprehend this situation. Government and social order were contrivances devised for them through their own reason and sense experience to improve this situation. It was a subordinate practical convenience, not a focus of value in itself. The most arrogant of rulers (and one should remember that some seventeenth century rulers were not beyond equating their own persons with the state)[24] were nothing more than practical conveniences for ordinary men and women. And the religious beliefs of all

22 John Dunn, *The Political Thought of John Locke*, Cambridge 1969.
23 Dunn, *Political Thought of Locke*, caps. 14 & 18.
24 For somewhat diverging views of the implications of the famous (but perhaps apocryphal) formula 'L'État c'est moi' attributed to the youthful Louis XIV, cf. Herbert H. Rowen, 'L'État c'est à moi: Louis XIV and the State', *French Historical Studies*, II, 1, Spring 1961, pp. 83–98; and 'Louis XIV and Absolutism', in John C. Rule (ed.), *Louis XIV and the Craft of Kingship*, Columbus, Ohio 1969, pp. 302–16; with William F. Church, 'Louis XIV and Reason of State' in Rule (ed.), *op. cit.*, pp. 363–406. For the development of ideological opposition to the absolutism of Louis in France itself see Lionel Rothkrug, *Opposition to Louis XIV: the Political and Social Origins of the French Enlightenment*, Princeton, N. J. 1965. For the emergence of absolutist political theory see Julian H. Franklin, *Jean Bodin and the Rise of Absolutist Theory*, Cambridge 1973. For absolutism as a state form see especially Anderson, *Lineages of the Absolutist State*.

men (or, more accurately, of all except Roman Catholics and atheists)[25] were fully entitled to be tolerated because believing in God is something which one can only in principle do for oneself, as an individual; and an imposed conformity of doctrine and observance was thus not only absurd and pointless but also an offence against the central value of religious authenticity.

Locke was the sort of liberal that he was because he saw those political and social values as rational interpretations of God's requirements for men. Christian revelation and the god-given capacity for rational understanding gave all men who bothered to make the effort a clear grasp of how they should live their lives. The core of confidence around which Locke arranged his liberal values and which made sense of these was a confidence in the availability to all men (or at least to all Christians) of viable shapes of individual life, vocations or callings.[26] Reductive egoistic liberalism in Locke's case then turns out to be predicated on an explicitly transcendental and extra-human order of value. But, even more oddly, when Locke does consider, for a fleeting moment, what the human condition would be, if this extra-human authority were removed, the language which he speaks is not the language of stolid bourgeois utility but the flashier and more aesthetic language of existential self-creation: 'A dependent intelligent being,' he wrote, 'is under the power and direction and dominion of him on whom he depends and must be for the ends appointed him by that superior being. If man were independent he could have no law but his own will, no end but himself. He would be a god to himself and the satisfaction of his own will the sole measure and end of all his actions.'[27] He would be a god to himself – and so, when God in due course died, man, an intelligent being, no longer aware of any other being on whom he *was* dependent, set himself to try to be. What gave Locke the nerve to be a reductive egoistic liberal, we may say, was a somewhat supine religious conviction, which if it had been effectively threatened would have left him not a stolid spokesman of bourgeois capitalist social achievements but a morally anarchic exponent of individual self-creation, a somewhat doleful Nietzschean, way before his time.

Liberal thought did *not*, however, remain theological in its base for

25 John Locke, *Epistola'de Tolerantia*, ed. & tr. R. Klibansky & J. W. Gough, Oxford 1968, pp. 130–5.
26 See Dunn, *Political Thought of Locke*, esp. caps. 18 & 19.
27 John Locke, *Ethica B* (Locke Mss, Bodleian Library, C28 p. 141) (quoted from Dunn, *Political Thought of Locke*, p. 1.)

very long. By the early nineteenth century British utilitarian political theory was determinedly secular in its intellectual allegiance.[28] Bentham and James Mill saw a liberal individualist politics as a logical outcome of the broad intellectual methods authenticated by the progress of natural science. A mechanical conception of human nature, an egoistic psychology, a purely instrumental interpretation of the character of social and political relations, were all the proper outcome of the scientific attitude towards man's place in society and in nature. They were the product of a rational interpretation of experience and an experientially grounded conception of reason. Push-pin *was au fond* as good as poetry, if men happened to find it so.[29] Whatever was on balance preferred was right. A mode of understanding which had proved astonishingly powerful in its application to nature and which accorded comfortably enough with some of the organizational features of capitalist society was stretched to encompass the whole of human existence,[30] banishing as its exponents hoped superstition, but banishing at the same time and as the price of this demystification the conviction that human existence had any particular purpose or perhaps at worst even any particular *point*. The political aspects of James Mill's and Bentham's thought were, on the whole, liberal enough. At least in the later parts of both of their lives, they advocated a fairly democratic form of responsible government; and Bentham at least in many ways managed to sustain emotionally the bewilderingly stringent intellectual implications for tolerance which followed from the view that all human desires of equivalent force, whatever their direction and character, were in themselves strictly morally on a par.[31] If there have ever been paradigms of reductive mechanical liberalism, Bentham and James Mill must qualify for the title.[32] And it seems a

---

28 The best treatment of the development of this intellectual movement as a whole remains Elie Halévy, *The Growth of Philosophic Radicalism*, tr. M. Morris, London 1928.
29 Cf. John Stuart Mill's dismayed commentary in his essay on Bentham (John Stuart Mill, *Essays on Politics and Culture*, ed. Gertrude Himmelfarb, pb. ed. Garden City, New York 1963, pp. 117–18.)
30 For an interesting account of the development of this style of thinking see Leszek Kolakowski, *Positivist Philosophy: From Hume to the Vienna Circle*, tr. N. Guterman, pb. ed. Harmondsworth 1972.
31 For accounts of Bentham which bring this characteristic out well see Mary P. Mack, *Jeremy Bentham: An Odyssey of Ideas 1748–1792*, London 1962 and James Steintrager, *Bentham*, pb. ed. London 1977. For a vivid attack on less rigorously liberal features of his thought see Gertrude Himmelfarb, *Victorian Minds*, London 1968, pp. 32–81: 'The Haunted House of Jeremy Bentham'.
32 Cf. Alan Ryan, 'Two Concepts of Politics and Democracy: James and John Stuart Mill'

reasonable historical judgement – particularly in view of both of their contributions to classical economics – to explain their confidence in the validity of their political conclusions not just in terms of the cultural triumph of the positivist mode of thought but in terms of the dynamic economic progress of capitalism in Britain at the time. Indeed both Bentham and James Mill made in fact perfectly explicit both their confidence in the political viability of capitalist society in ideological terms and their own conviction of the homogeneity of interest throughout the membership of capitalist society.[33]

To underline in this way the external character of the guarantee of their theory's political terms is to make apparent that both its reductive and mechanical qualities and its psychological egoism could readily sustain a very different politics. A less complacent economic theory or a less settled assurance of the ideological hegemony of bourgeois values – and consequently a less settled assurance of the *political* viability of capitalist society – could easily generate a politics which only the very dogmatic would be likely to christen 'liberal' at all. In the hands of Thomas Hobbes, for example, a somewhat earlier version of the natural scientific perspective on politics was certainly irreproachably individualist in its terms, certainly as fierce in its insistence on irreducible human egoism, certainly as ruthless in its reduction of humanity to matter and motion as any early nineteenth century utilitarian; and it was also, if anything, even more eloquent in its assault on superstition. But the political conclusions which followed from it, as set out in *Leviathan* in 1651,[34] were as autocratic, as illiberal as one could well imagine. If Locke trusted in God, and Bentham and James Mill trusted in capitalism, Hobbes trusted intellectually in nothing whatever but his own intelligence and the rigours of Euclidean geometry; and he trusted *politically* and existentially only in that minimal level of human rationality requisite to avoid collective suicide. So far from regarding toleration as a public duty or an individual right, he explicitly claimed the right for the public authority to impose the overt recognition of whatever beliefs it fancied upon its subject population. Thinking for themselves and judging for themselves as individuals was a social practice which – in all but rulers – Hobbes vehemently

in Martin Fleisher (ed.), *Machiavelli and the Nature of Political Thought*, London 1973, pp. 76–113.

33 See above chapter 1, note 54.

34 For a clear presentation of Hobbes's political thought as a whole see M. M. Goldsmith, *Hobbes's Science of Politics*, New York 1966.

deplored. He saw the great bulk of his contemporaries as fantasy-crazed loons, deluding themselves that they were the recipients of divine inspiration. When the Bible was translated into English, as he bitterly complained, 'every man, nay, every boy and wench, that could read English, thought they spoke with God Almighty, and understood what he said'.[35] Hobbes's radical individualism was a device for dispersing social superstition – for penetrating behind collective delusions to what was palpably and undeniably there – for bringing men quite literally back to their senses. But it was hardly based on *confidence* in any aspect of society or history whatever. The political conclusions to which it led were the very reverse of liberal and the values which it affirmed, insofar as it *affirmed* any values whatever, are scarcely values which one could call 'liberal' in common speech. Taken all in all, the relation between a reductive and mechanical egoism and liberal politics begins to look fairly historically contingent.

Reductive liberalism takes individuals as its basic conceptual units precisely because they are the smallest units to which human society can be reduced and still remain in any way recognizably *human* society. But such material reducibility hardly in itself provides much ground for *respecting* the individual residue. Individuals might be all that, humanly speaking, was there; but this consideration alone would scarcely give one grounds for treating them as a commanding focus of value, or for acknowledging a duty to tolerate their idiosyncratic tastes and opinions. Tolerance and respect for persons are liberal values which plainly require a less constricted account of what it is to be a human person than this provides if they are to be sustained at all convincingly. In Locke's day, as we saw, this fuller account was set firmly in a comprehensive religious theory of God's purposes for man. As historians we may well see the shadowy frame of this Christian ideological inheritance standing behind subsequent and more secular attempts to display the force of these values. On the whole the more secular apologists of tolerance and respect for persons have based their case upon a conception of the claims of reason.

35 Thomas Hobbes, *Behemoth or the Long Parliament*, ed F. Tönnies, 2nd ed. London 1969, p. 21. For interesting discussions of the social and political bearing of Hobbes's writings see: Keith Thomas, 'The Social Origins of Hobbes's Political Thought', in K. C. Brown (ed.), *Hobbes Studies*, Oxford 1965, pp. 185–236; Quentin Skinner, 'The Ideological Context of Hobbes's Political Thought', *The Historical Journal*, IX, 3, September 1966, pp. 286–317; and 'Conquest and Consent: Thomas Hobbes and the Engagement Controversy', in G. E. Aylmer (ed.), *The Interregnum*, London 1972, pp. 79–98; Richard Ashcraft, 'Ideology and Class in Hobbes's Political Theory', *Political Theory*, VI, 1, February 1978, pp. 27–62.

Liberalism

There have been two main varieties of case developed: one which is
based, as with Rousseau and Kant, very firmly on a view of the place of
reason within the individual moral life; and a second, less fundamentally hostile to empiricism and perhaps best articulated by John Stuart
Mill, which is based essentially on a view of reason's part in the social
development of veridical understanding: that is, on a philosophy of
science. Neither Rousseau nor Kant nor even John Stuart Mill are
particularly transparent and simple thinkers; and to see how their
conceptions of reason relate to liberal values, it will be necessary to
caricature their thought pretty drastically. Broadly, one may say, both
Rousseau and Kant[36] took a view of the nature of morality which
placed the individual will, the moral self, at its centre. As heirs of
European Protestant Christianity they saw the central value of the
moral life as that of responsibility and the central conceptual puzzle of
moral theory as the reconciliation between the value of responsibility
and the place of man as a natural being within the causal order of
nature. Reductive mechanical liberals have on the whole capitulated
imaginatively to the vision of man as causally incorporated within a
uniform natural causality – as placed firmly *within* nature. Rousseau
and Kant were both extremely sensitive to the causal character of
human sentiment, the degree to which it is socially and psychologically *moulded*. But instead of evacuating the concept of responsibility
with more or less relief from the spheres of morality, they chose
instead to elevate it to a dizzy eminence over this sphere. The central
duty of the individual moral life, according to both Rousseau and Kant,
the *formal* duty which divided off true morality from contingent causal
good or ill fortune, was, to put it somewhat facetiously, the rigorous
confrontation of causality by the individual will. A Kantian moral
agent, when acting morally, acted consciously and with integrity,
assumed total responsibility for the character of his act and, in doing
so, put natural causality firmly in its place. What enabled a human
being in this way to transcend natural causality was his capacity to
reason, an ability to grasp formal relations. The form of a good act for
an individual was – very roughly – an act performed in such a manner
that the individual could will that act to be a universal law (a require-

36 For the common features of Rousseau's and Kant's conception of morality see
especially Ernst Cassirer, *The Question of Jean-Jacques Rousseau*, tr. Peter Gay, pb. ed.
Bloomington, Ind. 1963; and Ernst Cassirer, *Rousseau, Kant and Goethe*, tr. J. Gut-
mann, P. Kristeller & J. H. Randall, pb. ed. New York 1963, pp. 1–60. For the core of
Kant's conception of the role of reason in man's ethical life seen his *Fundamental
Principles of the Metaphysic of Morals*, tr. T. K. Abbott, pb. ed. Indianapolis 1949.

44

ment fundamentally of evaluative consistency).[37] And the key precondition for an individual to perform such acts was the condition of autonomy, the full assumption of responsibility for one's own moral life. Working through these values in a simple-minded fashion, the duty of individual autonomy readily implies the right to individual autonomy; and an individual's right to individual autonomy plainly implies their duty to respect the autonomy of others. The right and duty of tolerance and the requirement of respect for persons are clearly enough established. But there remain very apparent difficulties.

Firstly there is the very queasy conceptual compatibility between the categorical notion of autonomy and any view of man's relation to natural causality.[38] And secondly (and perhaps more damagingly for the politics of liberalism) there is the unnervingly unanchored quality of the status attributed to these fine liberal values. One can see readily enough the historical basis of Rousseau and Kant's own convictions. But to do so merely accentuates the extreme cultural contingency of these convictions, their abject dependence on the historical Christian solidity of early modern European society. If we examine their political specification by Rousseau and Kant themselves, the results are almost equally discouraging. Kant's domestic politics seem merely archaic and fusty,[39] while Rousseau's are either simply irrelevant to the circumstances of modern societies[40] or, if drastically mis-interpreted into relevance, highly illiberal in their implications.[41] And if we both remove some of the cultural contingency and disregard their authors' own political interpretations of what the values required, the residual basis of the relations between autonomy, morality and reason seems wholly inadequate to sustain viable principles of practical life. Christianity takes individuals so seriously because they have souls and because the significance of these plainly transcends the significance of any value set upon individuals as members of society. But it seems a

37 Kant, *Fundamental Principles*, p. 55: 'Therefore, every rational being must so act as if he were by his maxims in every case a legislating member in the universal kingdom of ends. The formal principle of these maxims is: So act as if thy maxim were to serve likewise as the universal law (of all rational beings).'
38 A bold (if not in the end very persuasive) attempt to specify how these notions can appropriately be seen as compatible is Martin Hollis, *Models of Man: Philosophical Thoughts on Social Action*, Cambridge 1977.
39 For sympathetic accounts of Kant as a political thinker see the editor's introduction to *Kant's Political Writings*, ed. Hans Reiss, Cambridge 1971 and Georges Vlachos, *La Pensée politique de Kant*, Paris 1962.
40 See Judith Shklar, *Men and Citizens*, Cambridge 1968.
41 Much of J. L. Talmon's *The Origins of Totalitarian Democracy*, pb. ed. London 1961 may be read instructively in this sense.

reasonable judgement that Christianity is conceptually able to attribute such an over-riding weight to the significance of the individual's possession of a soul simply and solely because a soul is something which he possesses strictly *in addition to* all his attributes as a member of society. But human reason, whatever peculiar ontological realms it can give an individual access to, can hardly in principle be in this way a *supplement* to the full set of his attributes as a member of society. As members of society, men are already to the best of their achieved abilities, rational creatures. The possession of a soul can be a wholly external characteristic of man as a member of society. As the possessor of a soul a man can put his own society or any other society very firmly in its place. It is much less clear how far he may do the same simply as the possessor of reason. We can draw a lesson perhaps from seeing the consequences of attempting to derive a modern ethical theory from the formal rationality criterion of Kantian ethics, an attempt undertaken by Professor R. M. Hare.[42] In the resulting doctrine, morality, conceptually a socially shared and etymologically even a *public customary* affair, is transposed into an affair of purely individualist arbitrariness, constrained solely by the formal requirement of consistency. It is hard to see a conceptual heritage which fails in this way to generate any substantive social morality at all[43] furnishing an adequate defence for such demanding and naturally counter-intuitive cultural values as the duty of autonomy and the right to tolerance.

None of this commentary, of course, is very novel. Already in the early nineteenth century Hegel was insisting on the inadequacy of seeing reason as an individual faculty which gave access to an order of transcendent truths and insisting instead on the need to see it as a socially dependent capability, a cultural artefact: knower and known as a conspiracy of cultures.[44] And if reason was a social capacity, as

42 See R. M. Hare, *The Language of Morals*, Oxford 1952 and *Freedom and Reason*, Oxford 1963. For a historical placing of Hare's thinking see Alasdair Macintyre, *A Short History of Ethics*, pb. ed. New York 1966, cap. 18.

43 See especially R. M. Hare, 'The Lawful Government' in Peter Laslett & W. G. Runciman (eds.), *Philosophy, Politics and Society, 3rd Series*, Oxford 1967, pp. 157–72. Two important works which employ a rather less spare conception of reason in the articulation and defence of political values (but which also pay a measure of homage to Kant) are the works by Rawls and Nozick discussed in note 50 below.

44 The key work in which this conception was first set out and published *in extenso* is *The Phenomenology of Spirit* [*Geist*] (1807). This is an exceptionally difficult work to grasp even in outline. For a variety of attempts to introduce the novice to Hegel's thinking see J. N. Findlay, *Hegel: A Re-examination*, London 1958; Walter Kaufmann, *Hegel: Reinterpretation, Texts and Commentary*, London 1966 (with helpful biographical information); Charles Taylor, *Hegel*, Cambridge 1975; Raymond Plant, *Hegel*, pb. ed. London 1973.

Hegel and Marx and a variety of more modern epistemologists[45] have all insisted (if for very different reasons), it was no longer easy to see how the claims of individuals could serve as a commanding external standard to which society must endlessly, as best it could, measure up. If individuals themselves were cultural artefacts, social products, trapped once again within a relentless causality, though now a sociological and no longer a homogeneous natural causality, it was hard to see how they could have valid claims to a measure of tolerance very much more extensive than the majority of their society felt on the whole inclined to give them. Hegel and Marx, of course, were both after their fashion deeply committed to the principle of subjectivity.[46] But the liaison between tolerance and sociological causality in their thought can readily in retrospect look like the product of a simple affection for times past. Certainly the intellectual and political progeny of either, whether legitimate or illegitimate, have made it drastically apparent that the link is by no means one of conceptual necessity.

In the face of this threat there are two possible radical intellectual strategies open to those who aspire to rescue liberalism as a coherent political option, both of them necessarily somewhat perilous. One is to shrink liberalism to a more or less pragmatic and sociological doctrine about the relations between types of political and social order and the enjoyment of political liberties. The version of liberalism which embraces this option most openly is what is usually today termed 'pluralism', a conception which reaches back to Montesquieu and de

45 See, for example, in very different ways: T. S. Kuhn, *The Structure of Scientific Revolutions*, Chicago 1962; Imre Lakatos & Alan Musgrave (eds.), *Criticism and the Growth of Knowledge*, Cambridge 1970; Paul Feyerabend, *Against Method*, pb. ed. London 1978; W. V. O. Quine, *Word and Object*, pb. ed. 1964; W. V. O. Quine, *From a Logical Point of View*, 2nd ed. pb. New York 1963, cap. II, 'Two Dogmas of Empiricism', pp. 20–46; W. V. O. Quine & J. S. Ullian, *The Web of Belief*, pb. ed. New York 1970; Hilary Putnam, *Meaning and the Moral Sciences*, London 1978; Louis Althusser & Étienne Balibar, *Reading Capital*, tr. B. Brewster, pb. ed. London 1975. Perhaps the main problem in modern philosophy of science is to distinguish the grounds for supposing that human cognition is socially dependent (a historically informed view) from grounds for concluding that it is in some sense socially constituted (an explicitly relativist view). For striking presentations of these issues see Bernard Williams, 'The Truth in Relativism', in *Proceedings of the Aristotelian Society*, 1975, pp. 215–28 and *Descartes: The Project of Pure Enquiry*, pb. ed. Harmondsworth 1978 and Putnam, *op. cit.*

46 For Hegel see above chapter 1 note 45. In the case of Marx the judgement is now controversial: cf. Althusser & Balibar, *Reading Capital*. For a patient and lucid exegesis of the divergence at the epistemological level between Althusser's dogmatic repudiation of the category of the human subject and Marx's project of the self-emancipation of the proletariat see Susan James's fine *Holism in Social Theory: The Case of Marxism*, University of Cambridge PhD thesis 1978.

Tocqueville, whose most vigorous contemporary European exponent is the sociologist Raymond Aron[47] and which is still in effect the official intellectual ideology of American society.[48] The second possible radical strategy is simply to repudiate the claims of sociology, to take an epistemological position of such stark scepticism that the somewhat over-rated causal status of sociology can safely be viewed with un-limited scorn. The political implications of this doctrine tend to be fairly cursory. But if it treats politics seriously enough to bother to spell out implications for it at all, these tend to constitute a form of extreme individualist anarchism, if not indeed of nihilism. Besides these two radical solutions, there has been at least one famous attempt to synthe-size the two and indeed even to conflate them with the reductive mechanical individualism of the British empirical tradition, the thought of James Mill's hapless son, John Stuart Mill. The attempt to integrate intellectual traditions so deeply and explicitly inimical to one another was not in principle a very promising one in prospect; and it certainly did not belie this lack of promise in its actual execution. But it was a strikingly brave attempt and some of the discrete fragments of thought which it left behind it still have a notable power to move the imaginations (or at least the feelings) of those who find liberal values attractive. I shall end accordingly by discussing briefly each of these three responses.

Pluralism is the least interesting of the three, if undoubtedly the most influential. Its relevant intellectual career begins with the French Ancien Regime of the eighteenth century in which the nobility defended their property rights in state office and in residual feudal privileges over the rest of the population under the banner of the French Constitution, presenting themselves as the sole effective defenders of the legal rights and civil liberties of the entire French population.[49] Their most famous apologist, the Bordeaux magistrate Montesquieu, portrayed the existence of independent social forces

47 Aron is a prolific writer and a determined exponent of the integrity and continuity of this tradition. See for example his *Main Currents of Sociological Thought*, tr. R. Howard & H. Weaver, 2 vols., pb. ed. Harmondsworth 1968–70; *The Opium of the Intellectuals*, tr. T. Kilmartin, pb. ed. New York 1962; *The Industrial Society*, London 1967. For an interesting discussion of the relation between Montesquieu and de Tocqueville see Melvin Richter, 'The Uses of Theory: Tocqueville's adaptation of Montesquieu', in M. Richter (ed), *Essays in Theory and History*, Cambridge, Mass. 1970, pp. 74–102.
48 See chapter 1 note 63 above.
49 See e.g. Franklin L. Ford, *Sword and Robe*, Cambridge, Mass. 1953, esp. cap. XII. E. Carcassonne, *Montesquieu et le problème de la constitution française au XVIIIe siècle*, Paris 1927.

outside the control of the French crown, *'pouvoirs intermédiaires'* as he called them, as the sole durably effective barrier in eighteenth century Europe to the establishment of centralized despotic power. This thesis, the *thèse nobiliare* as it was termed, was opposed by an alternative doctrine, emanating from the reforming ministers of the royal court, the *thèse royale*, which portrayed the position of the French nobility within the Ancien Regime, accurately enough, as the crude exploitation of arbitrary privilege and the systematic obstruction of rationalizing reform in the direction of citizen equality, economic efficiency and social justice. It was the drastically effective centralization of the French revolutionary regime and its Napoleonic successor which really lent intellectual depth to the *thèse nobiliaire*, even after the political demise of the nobility themselves. In response to this experience – and in the hands of Alexis de Tocqueville – it became an effective critique of the entire political strategy of realizing liberal goals by concentrating power within the state apparatus. In its late twentieth century American version, pluralism is now the doctrine that the social preconditions for enduring political liberty and cultural freedom involve a highly self-subsistent civil society, a civil society which is in some real measure independent of the state apparatus. The political core of liberalism is here seen as responsible government embellished with civil liberties; and responsible government is seen as presupposing a society with sufficient capacity for self-organization, sufficient autonomy, to *hold* a government effectively responsible to itself. Modern pluralism is thus at least sufficiently sociologically self-aware not to blench from the insight that a liberal polity is the political form of bourgeois capitalist society. But the price which it has paid, so far pretty willingly, for this self-awareness, is the surrender of any plausible overall intellectual frame, uniting epistemology, psychology and political theory, which explains and celebrates the force of such political commitment.[50] The

50 The nearest to a comprehensive liberal theory at present available is the conception set out by two distinguished émigré scholars, Karl Popper and F. A. Hayek. The core of their views is an insistence on the intimate dependence of the progress of human rationality on a particular way of organizing society, one which acknowledges the necessary epistemological frailty of all human authority and the limited intelligibility in detail (and hence the limited possibilities of controlling in a fully intended manner the organization) of human society. As an economist Hayek lays more stress on the economic efficacy of the market mechanism, while the philosopher Popper by contrast emphasizes predominantly the perils of excessive confidence in the validity of their own understanding (and excessive power to implement this understanding) on the part of those who rule. Neither thinker offers a very robust conception of the character of the creatures (human beings) whose freedom and rationality they wish to

transcendent, self-expressive, morally intense individualism of bourgeois society at its apogee is here thrust back all too firmly and anxiously into purely private life. Pluralism is the political theory of bourgeois society up against the wall.

Individualist anarchism or nihilism certainly offer a response which is more interesting than pluralism. But they do so in effect by espousing the fantasy that perhaps there might come to be nothing but purely private life, an idea even more implausible than, though perhaps not as menacing as, the prospect that there might come to be nothing but

defend; and neither shows much understanding of the social and economic causation of the steady collapse of the form of liberal society which they hold dear. For Popper see particularly *The Poverty of Historicism*, 2nd ed., London 1960; *The Open Society and its Enemies*, 3rd ed. 2 vols., London 1957; and *The Logic of Scientific Discovery*, tr. by the author & J. & L. Freed, 6th ed. London 1972. For Hayek see *The Counter-Revolution of Science*, pb. ed. New York 1964; *New Studies in Philosophy, Politics, Economics and the History of Ideas*; and *The Constitution of Liberty*, London 1960. Despite the integrity and the intellectual force of some aspects of their writing, these two lacunae make their theoretical position altogether thinner and more politically peripheral than that of such predecessors as Thomas Hobbes, John Locke or David Hume.

Most recent pluralist political theory rests fairly banally at the level of vulgar politics and offers no intellectually coherent conception of human value at all. But there have been two striking and much discussed recent attempts by American philosophers to resuscitate liberal political theory which deserve mention. One of these, John Rawls, *A Theory of Justice*, pb. ed. London 1973, seeks to derive strong normative principles of social organization from a conception of what it would be rational for genuinely culturally and pragmatically impartial human beings to choose. This work has not stood up at all convincingly to criticism. It remains dubious whether human beings who were rendered sufficiently rigorously impartial could intelligibly and rationally *choose* at all and equally dubious whether, if they could do so (and could be expected to settle on a single determinate set of choices), their prospective choices would bear any normative significance at all for actual (partial) human beings. It is also difficult to see, whatever its merits within the theory of criminal justice, that an adequate conception of social justice could afford to allot such overwhelming conceptual weight to the idea of impartiality and such little conceptual weight to experientially grounded social imagination. For a variety of attacks on Rawls's arguments see Brian Barry, *The Liberal Idea of Justice*, pb. ed. Oxford 1973; Norman Daniels (ed.), *Reading Rawls: Critical Studies of a Theory of Justice*, pb. ed. Oxford 1975; David Miller, *Social Justice*, Oxford 1976. The second work, Robert Nozick's *Anarchy, State and Utopia*, Oxford 1975 defends a conception of social justice within which purely private life occupies a generous proportion of the moral space available to human existence in its entirety. The argument is premised upon an ideologically bathetic (and culturally parochial) conception of human rights, introduced virtually without discussion. (See the review by John Dunn, *Ratio*, XIX, 1, June 1977, pp. 88–95.) Both of these texts are works of great philosophical accomplishment. But neither is informed with any coherent understanding of the social, political and economic realities of most of the world today and neither presents a philosophically defensible conception of the epistemological foundations of ethical theory. For a helpful placing of the two see John N. Gray, 'Social Contract, Community and Ideology', in Pierre Birnbaum, Jack Lively & Geraint Parry (eds.), *Democracy, Consensus and Contract*, London 1978, pp. 225–43.

purely public life.[51] Their individualism is indeed splendid in its transcendence, in the vigour of its self-expression and perhaps, in an obscure fashion, even in its moral intensity. But it leaves them confronting History in the classic pose of the ostrich. Max Stirner, the Left Hegelian author of *The Ego and His Own*, summed up the politics of pure individuality in a memorable if derivative apothegm: 'the egoist . . . has nothing to say to the State except "Get out of my sunshine."' [52] This response showed a spectacular and undeniably impressive effrontery when – as the legend has it – Diogenes the Cynic addressed it from the depths of his barrel to Alexander the Great in person.[53] But it hardly has the same resonance when muttered at large at the modern pluralist democracy. And since it is so plainly the case that modern states are going to continue to have more than this to say in reply to the egoist, it looks a little thin as a political programme.

In contrast to these stark and implausible alternatives, John Stuart Mill's thought appears considerably more amorphous. If one looks over the works as a whole, there are, it is true, certain broad consistencies of purpose and intellectual disposition;[54] and in part the air of

51 A more politically exigent version of anarchist theory which is not committed to any particular view about social causation or social possibility is to be found in Robert Paul Wolff, *In Defence of Anarchism*, 2nd pb. ed. New York 1976. Wolff argues, on the basis of a Kantian conception of moral responsibility, that no categories of social and political membership can excuse the individual on every occasion from judging the moral propriety of political commands for him- or her-self and thus that there cannot be legitimate political authority. It is at least intelligible how this conclusion can be derived from a Kantian ethical viewpoint (though it differs fairly starkly from the conclusions which Kant himself drew). But Wolff offers no defence of the ethical theory as such within this text; and, if the conclusion is indeed validly derived, it looks extremely like a *reductio ad absurdum* of the ethical theory. States being what they are, moral vigilance is no doubt morally prudent. But how precisely are individuals to be presumed to derive their title to exercise such hysterical fastidiousness on the entire framework of practices which makes their existence (as they actually are) possible at all?

52 Max Stirner, *The Ego and his Own*, ed. John Carroll, London 1971, p. 156. For studies of Stirner see R. W. K. Paterson, *The Nihilistic Egoist: Max Stirner*, London 1971; Eugène Fleischmann, 'The role of the individual in pre-revolutionary society: Stirner, Marx and Hegel', in Z. A. Pelczynski (ed.), *Hegel's Political Philosophy: Problems and Perspectives*, Cambridge 1971, pp. 220–9; Karl Löwith, *From Hegel to Nietzsche: The Revolution in Nineteenth Century Thought*, London 1964.

53 "ἀποσκότησόν μου', Diogenes Laertius, *Lives of Eminent Philosophers*, Bk VI, 38, Loeb edition, tr. R. D. Hicks, London 1925, Vol. 2, pp. 40–1 (Life of Diogenes). The legend is probably apocryphal: see e.g. W. W. Tarn, *Alexander the Great*, Cambridge 1948, Vol. 2, p. 405. D. R. Dudley, *A History of Cynicism from Diogenes to the Sixth Century AD*, London 1937, p. 17.

54 For helpful treatments which bring out such unity as his thought does possess see Alan Ryan, *The Philosophy of John Stuart Mill*, London 1970 and *J. S. Mill*, pb. ed. London 1974.

incoherence which surrounds the body of the work taken as a whole is simply a product of the very broad range over which Mill attempted to make up his mind. The *System of Logic*, the *Principles of Political Economy*, *Utilitarianism*, *On Liberty*, the *Considerations on Representative Government*, the *Subjection of Women*, the *Three Essays on Religion*, constitute an amazingly wide array of topics on which for a single thinker to attempt a systematic judgement; and when we add in the range of sociological and political issues surveyed in the *Dissertations and Discussions*, to say nothing of the *Autobiography*, a measure of disarray is scarcely surprising. But the weakness which matters in Mill's thought is less the absence of consistent overall intellectual control, than a number of fundamental tensions between the values to which he *is* fully committed. Starting off optimistically in the endeavour to unite the intellectual virtues of Bentham and Coleridge,[55] a level-headed empirical rigour with a less impoverished, more aesthetic and more sociologically adequate conception of human personality, Mill ended up with no coherent conception of human personality at all. In the *Considerations on Representative Government* he managed to combine without apparent intellectual distress an account of the purposes of government as a mechanism for reducing mutual risks between individuals with a doctrine of the individual civic life which insisted on the primacy of politics as a field for individual moral self-development and an interpretation of the vote as the conscientious passing of a verdict on the merits of a political case, which it would be as reprehensible to tinge with considerations of individual interest as the decision of a juryman in a criminal trial.[56] In *On Liberty*,[57] his most famous and still his most controversial work, he argued vigorously for the right of the non-maleficent individual to non-interference from the acts of others,

55 See the essays on Bentham and Coleridge: John Stuart Mill, *Essays on Politics and Culture*, caps. III & IV. John Stuart Mill, *Autobiography*, London 1924, cap. V.
56 John Stuart Mill, *Considerations on Representative Government*, Everyman ed. London 1910; risk reduction 194–5, 258–60, 276–7, 289; participation 207–9, 217–18, 243, 278–9; cf p. 299: 'no person can have a right (except in the purely legal sense) to power over others: every such power, which he is allowed to possess, is morally, in the fullest force of the term, a trust. . . . His vote is not a thing in which he has an option; it has no more to do with his personal wishes than the verdict of a juryman. It is strictly a matter of duty; he is bound to give it according to his best and most conscientious opinion of the public good. Whoever has any other idea of it is unfit to have the suffrage'; For a clear and careful assessment of the *Considerations* see Dennis F. Thompson, *John Stuart Mill and Representative Government*, Princeton, N. J. 1976.
57 *On Liberty* remains the most controversial of Mill's writings and its correct interpretation is thus vividly disputed. For a balanced account see Ryan, *J. S. Mill*, cap. 5 and esp. p. 132.

a natural right if ever there was one – but one which Mill himself was precluded from presenting as such by the authority of Bentham (who dismissed natural rights as 'simple nonsense')[58] and which Mill set himself to defend instead in strictly consequentialist terms by an exceptionally feeble argument as to the necessary economic, cultural and political cost of encroaching in any way on freedom of speech. Because Mill was so ambivalent in his sense of what an individual actually amounted to, he could not base his defence of a right to tolerance on any strong conception of individual personality and what aspects of this might be judged to require respect. Instead he was obliged to weave nervously together a reasonably plausible argument taken from his philosophy of science about the conditions for developing rational understanding, a strikingly implausible general theory of social change and a decidedly Romantic celebration of the cultural mission of the resolutely unpopular, especially among the intelligentsia. It was not a promising approach towards establishing any conclusion whatever; and it went no distance at all towards establishing the claim that no society or individual was ever justified in coercing another individual unless the latter had already in effect interfered with some other person.

Liberal values today are certainly still not without their attractions. Nor need we on balance regret being the heirs of a Christian Europe.

58 'Natural rights is simple nonsense – natural and imprescriptible rights, rhetorical nonsense – nonsense upon stilts.' The phrase comes from Bentham's critique of the 1791 Declaration of Rights (*Anarchical Fallacies being an Examination of the Declarations of Rights issued during the French Revolution, The Works of Jeremy Bentham*, ed. J. Bowring, Edinburgh 1843, Vol. 2, p. 501); and see the vehement assault on natural rights in *Supply without Burthen* (1795), in W. Stark (ed.), *Jeremy Bentham's Economic Writings*, Vol. I, London 1952, pp. 332–7, especially 337: 'Nonsense it always was from the beginning, but those upon whom it pressed, and who suffered themselves to be imposed upon while its malignity lay concealed, may now that its malignity has shewn itself in all its full blackness, perhaps suffer themselves to be weaned from it', and p. 336 'To speak these verbal daggers is to promise upon the first occasion to use real ones, and in that promise consists its force.' There is an interesting discussion of Bentham's attempts to demystify political language in J. H. Burns, 'Bentham's Critique of Political Fallacies', in Bhiku Parekh (ed.), *Jeremy Bentham: Ten Critical Essays*, London 1974, pp. 154–67; and a helpful account of the impact of the French Revolution upon his thinking in J. H. Burns, 'Bentham and the French Revolution', *Transactions of the Royal Historical Society*, 5th Series, Vol. XVI, 1966, pp. 95–114. For the damage inflicted on Bentham's own thought by the inadequacy of his conception of rights see H. L. A. Hart, 'Bentham', in Parekh (ed.), *Bentham Critical Essays*, pp. 73–95. Bentham himself employed on occasion arguments the foundations of which are difficult to distinguish from 'natural rights': see e.g. the claim that each person has 'an equal right' to 'all the happiness that he is capable of', quoted by James Steintrager, *Bentham*, p. 57.

But there seems every reason to doubt the possibility of a comprehensive and coherent *modern* philosophy of liberalism; and perhaps more disturbingly (though perhaps also consequently) there seems little reason to believe that the more attractive values of liberalism enjoy any privileged relation to the historical process. Indeed the question has now become not one of whether History is *committed* to liberalism or to some more splendid and transcendent apotheosis of liberalism – but rather one of whether History is likely to continue much longer even to tolerate it. Marx spoke in the *Critique of the Gotha Programme*, as we have already noted, of the future in which all the springs of cooperative wealth would flow more abundantly, when for the first time in history the narrow horizon of bourgeois right can be crossed.[59] Today it is no longer easy to see how we could as a species expect to cross that narrow horizon and remain securely on the far side.

And on a world scale – and perhaps even domestically (at least in the United Kingdom as it is still derisorily known) – it looks more and more to be a horizon which is not approaching at all, but rather drawing relentlessly further and further away.

59 See above chapter 2 note 21. For the social-democratic pressure towards this horizon in Great Britain in the twentieth century see T. H. Marshall, *Citizenship and Social Class*, Cambridge 1950 and T. H. Marshall, *Class, Citizenship and Social Development*, pb. ed. Garden City, New York 1965, caps. XII–XV. For the view that the continuation of such progress is incompatible with the preservation of capitalist society see for example (from the right), F. A. Hayek, *New Studies* and (from the left), Andrew Gamble and Paul Walton, *Capitalism in Crisis: Inflation and the State*, London 1976. The capacity of capitalist society to survive can readily be underestimated. Its capacity to survive and continue to *extend* effective social rights and economic benefits within a weak and structurally very highly constrained economy, on the other hand, was until recently greatly overestimated in Great Britain.

3

vvvvvvvvvvvvvvvvvvvvvvvvvvvvvvvvvvvvvvvvvvvvvvvvvvvvvvvvvvvvvvvvvvvvvvvvvv

Nationalism

'Duty requires that men should defend not just whatever country they choose but their own particular fatherland. This requirement is the criterion by which the ethical activity of all individuals is measured; it is the source of all the recognised *duties* and laws which are known to every individual, and the objective basis on which each individual's position rests. For there is no room in living reality for empty notions like that of pursuing goodness for its own sake.'

   G. W. F. Hegel, *Lectures on the Philosophy of World History: Introduction*. (1830 draft) (quoted from the edition translated by H. B. Nisbet, Cambridge 1975, p. 80).

Nationalism is the starkest political shame of the twentieth century, the deepest, most intractable and yet most unanticipated blot on the political history of the world since the year 1900. But it is also the very tissue of modern political sentiment, the most widespread, the most unthinking and the most immediate political disposition of all at least among the literate populations of the modern world. The degree to which its prevalence is still felt as a scandal is itself a mark of the unexpectedness of this predominance, of the sharpness of the check which it has administered to Europe's admiring Enlightenment vision of the Cunning of Reason. In nationalism at last, or so it at present seems, the Cunning of Reason has more than met its match. There are two key episodes which have caused this realization to sink in. The first was the abject collapse of the touted proletarian solidarism of the Second International in August 1914 in the face of the mobilization of the European powers for the First World War.[1] The second, a more arbitrary and disputable date on which to fix, was the Nazi Seizure of Power in 1933. It is a nice point which of these two episodes has generated the greater and more conclusive shock. Certainly Socialism

1 Georges Haupt, *Socialism and the Great War: The Collapse of the Second International*, Oxford 1972.

has never looked the same since the parties of Engels and of Jaurès slunk into line and agreed to defend their fatherlands against the aggression of the largely proletarian armies of their foes. Socialism in one country was a natural political outcome of a movement which had split so effortlessly *along* national lines, even if its principal and somewhat unwitting architect, Lenin, was the most savage critic of this proletarian fission. But if the fate of Socialism was the betrayal of a promise, the rise of Fascism and above all the Nazi regime were the realization of a threat and a threat so dreadful in some of its manifestations that it is still hard for us to take in the scale and extension of the evil actions which it made possible. When the counter-revolutionary theorist Joseph de Maistre wished to assail the leaders of the Terror of 1793 he could measure the enormity of their deeds by accusing them of bringing the mores of the Iroquois and the Algonquin[2] to the squares of Paris – bringing back natural man to the centre of civilization. When critics of the Soviet Union wished to pillory Stalin as a reversion to Russian barbarism they could describe him in a famous quip as Genghis Khan with a telephone. But even the most strained of historical metaphors has quailed at the task of characterizing Hitler.

There are of course other metaphors of the twentieth century as terrifying and perhaps in the end as shaming as those of nationalism – spectacular fears of the more or less literal detonation of the living space at least of industrial countries through the use of nuclear weapons or drabber, if not less hysterical, anxieties at the prospect of a steady destruction of the human habitat. But these are not as yet assemblages of steady choices backed by assured feelings and it remains hard to imagine their ever becoming such. Human life on earth may in fact terminate sooner rather than later and if it does so political agencies will have to share plenty of the blame for its doing so. But when and if it does do so, it will hardly be our collective choice.

Yet nationalism, by contrast, is very much our collective choice. It is the common idiom of contemporary political feeling, at least off parade. It is not necessarily an unthinking or a morally irresponsible feeling and it is a feeling which certainly has to compete with other political feelings. Why should it have come to be so dominant and why should we be so surprised, even so horrified at the extent of its prevalence?

2 *The Works of Joseph de Maistre*, tr. J. Lively, New York 1965, p. 296.

Nationalism

It is easier to see a clear and convincing answer to the second question than it is to the first. If we are most of us nationalists in some measure now, we are certainly not necessarily insensitive to claims of supra-national human solidarities and we are still more certainly most of us not at all like Nazis. Nationalism for most of us is not an exhilarating emotional commitment but simply a habit of accommodation of which we feel the moral shabbiness readily enough ourselves. And it is hard for us altogether to lose sight of this shabbiness, just because nationalism does violate so directly the official conceptual categories of modern ethics, the universalist heritage of a natural law conceived either in terms of Christianity or of secular rationalism. The handbooks or official proclamations of this ethical heritage – from Samuel Pufendorf's seventeenth century *De Officio Hominis et Civis*[3] through the American Declaration of Independence of 1776 and the French Declaration of the Rights of Man and of the Citizen of 1789 to the United Nations Charter of our own day are intractably universalist. All of them take individual men, more or less as they are, as their fundamental ethical units and assess the legitimacy of possible laws or political arrangements in terms of the axiomatically identical rights which such men are presumed to possess. From the theory of justice suggested by scholastic philosophers in early modern Europe to that urged recently with such charm by John Rawls[4] there is no place for the nation or indeed for the sovereign political body as a unit of conceptual account. The rights of men are what lend to nations or states whatever rights these last can be properly accorded. Such other rights as they claim must be products simply of power, rights which they take and which they can hold, causal capabilities as Thrasymachus celebrated them in Plato's *Republic* and, as Plato himself insisted, facts which in themselves necessarily lack any trace of ethical authority.[5]

All this, of course, is a very Enlightenment way of thinking about the matter and a way which the intellectual heritage of nineteenth and early twentieth century Germany from the Romantics and Herder, through, at least from some points of view, the thought of Hegel, to the

3 Samuel von Pufendorf, *De Officio Hominis et Civis juxta Legem Naturalem Libri Duo*, ed. W. Schücking & tr. F. G. Moore, New York 1927. Carl L. Becker, *The Declaration of Independence. A Study in the History of Political Ideas*, pb. ed. New York 1958.
4 John Rawls, *A Theory of Justice*, pb. ed. London 1973.
5 *The Republic of Plato*, tr. Francis M. Cornford, Oxford 1941, pp. 14–39 (336B to 354C). A. W. H. Adkins, *Merit and Responsibility: A Study in Greek Values*, Oxford 1960, 258–93.

broad historicist sensibility of thinkers like Max Weber and Meinecke,[6] set itself to bury without trace. In response to the easy cosmopolitanism of the *Aufklärung*, historicist thought has boldly espoused the claims of the parochial, of cultural idiosyncracy and localism, of the folkways. The extent to which men vary according to time and place in the values which they hold dear and the projects which they pursue is seen theoretically as a species-specific characteristic of human beings as such and celebrated morally as the distinctive glory of the species. The universalist theory of the human species is that its destiny is to be intensely and necessarily particular.

There are, plainly, many extremely deep themes involved in this shift of intellectual and moral sensibility. What exactly, for example, are the relations between on the one hand the growing appreciation for the plurality of human cultures, a naturalist's joy in the astounding scope of human cultural differentiation and shame at the steady erosion of one endangered culture after another, and on the other hand the philosophical bemusements of ethical relativism – the view that all human values are in some sense specific to particular societies? And what connection is there between both of these shifts of intellectual sensibility and the pride of patriotism or the murderous shame of Fascist aggression and racist tyranny, the heroism of national resistance and liberation or the barbarism of genocide? One should not think even of the moral hesitancy at the triumph of new cultures as a wholly modern phenomenon, as though culturally in the past all communities were confidently Social Darwinist, if without knowing it. There is a beautiful passage in Walter Raleigh's *History of the World* written in prison at the very beginning of the seventeenth century which could serve as a perfect text for rescue ethnography today: 'the inventions of mortall men are no lesse mortall than themselves. The Fire, which the *Chaldaeans* worshipped for a God, is crept into every mans chimney, which the lacke of fuell starveth, water quencheth, and want of ayre suffocateth; *Jupiter* is no more vexed with Junoes jelousies; *Death* hath persuaded him to chastitie, and her to patience; and that

6 For Herder see especially Isaiah Berlin, *Vico and Herder*, London 1976, pp. 143–216 and F. M. Barnard, *Herder's Social and Political Thought: From Enlightenment to Nationalism*, Oxford 1965. For Hegel see especially Charles Taylor, *Hegel*, Cambridge 1975. For two illuminating perspectives on Weber's cultural relativism (and the limits of this) see W. G. Runciman, *A Critique of Max Weber's Philosophy of Social Science*, Cambridge 1972 and David Beetham, *Max Weber and the Theory of Modern Politics*, London 1974. For the historical context and the character of this transition in German thought as a whole see the works cited in note 35 below.

Time which hath devoured it selfe, hath also eaten up both the Bodies and Images of him and his: yea, their stately Temples of stone and durefull Marble. The houses and sumptuous buildings erected to *Baal*, can no where be found upon the earth; nor any monument of that glorious Temple consecrated to *Diana*. There are none now in *Phoenicia*, that lament the death of *Adonis*; nor any in *Libya*, *Creta*, *Thessalia*, or elsewhere, that ask counsaile or helpe from *Jupiter*. The great god *Pan* hath broken his pipes.'[7] To an at least partially Christian[8] renaissance intellectual like Raleigh the obliteration of the gods of the Ancient world by the Christian church militant was a process about which he could readily feel deeply in both directions. But the worship of Baal for example was not conducted in Greek or Latin and the point generalizes in any case with very little effort. All over the world today we can sense, if we will only listen for it, the Great God Pan breaking his pipes; and it is now open to us, as it was scarcely open to Raleigh, to see this process as the essence of human history – not the passage from Heathenism to faith, nor from Barbarism and superstition to civilization and rationality but the brutal natural selection of belief systems which are also always the site of meaning for the lives of real living men. To see human history this way is perhaps the essence of the historicist experience and it brings with it a condition which may perhaps be called – if a little solemnly – a state of hermeneutic ambivalence which is as imaginatively baffling as it is stimulating and which is both the central challenge facing any serious political theory today and a challenge which political theory at present is grotesquely failing to meet. We shall return very briefly to the significance of this state of hermeneutic ambivalence in the last chapter.

But it is not of course any such refined nostalgia for disappearing

7 Sir Walter Raleigh, *The History of the World*, London 1614, Bk I, cap. 6, para. viii, p. 96: 'That Heathenisme and Judaisme, after many wounds, were at length about the same time under JULIAN miraculously confounded.' For an assertion of continuity across this rift in a mildly startling context see J. E. McGuire & P. M. Rattansi, 'Newton and the "Pipes of Pan"', *Notes and Records of the Royal Society of London*, XXI, 2, December 1966, pp. 108–43.

8 For an elaborately argued case for seeing the Christian elements in Raleigh's expressed opinions simply in terms of 'impression-management' see Pierre Lefranc, *Sir Walter Raleigh écrivain: l'oeuvre et les idées*, Paris 1968, pp. 334–484, e.g. p. 484: 'En profondeur, le mouvement conduit Raleigh vers les platonismes et accessoirement vers la pensée libertine; en surface, il simule le puritanisme.' It is certainly true that Raleigh possessed an exceptionally histrionic temperament and that he took pleasure in shocking his contemporaries. But, on the evidence of the poetry and of his conduct during imprisonment in the Tower, it is hard to believe that the audience to which he was simulating a Puritan faith did not on occasion include himself.

folkways or savouring of the pathos of the extirpation of ancient creeds which presents an immediate practical threat in the union of historicist theory and nationalist political action. Affirming the folkways is all very well within the Folk; but it offers little grounds for optimism as a method of mediating between different folks. And in any case – What is my folk? – Which *is* my tribe? Or, as Captain Macmorris asks Fluellen in *Henry V*[9] – What is my nation? Too many self-righteous tribes within a single state can be in itself a recipe for genocide – in Uganda and Burundi of course, in Ethiopia today, in Nigeria all too recently, in South Africa perhaps all too soon.[10] Tribal or national self-righteousness does not merely produce, as previous ethical recipes have consistently tended to do, an excess of just wars. It also produces altogether too many situations in which there seems no longer to be any conceptual, let alone practical possibility of a just peace. Watching on our television screens, as we do, the hideous back streets of Belfast or the picturesque alleys of the old city of Jerusalem, it takes very little distance or imagination to see that almost anything would be better than what is likely to happen next in them. But even infinite distance and omniscience in the face of the tangled histories of massacre and cruelty which have led up to the present of these two cities would hardly suffice to reveal a future for either which would be at all transparently a just future.

If ethical relativism is the philosophical thesis that the mores of any tribe are as good as the mores of any other tribe – or more felicitously that it makes no sense to ask whether the mores of any tribe are *better* than the mores of any other tribe – because good and better are *defined intra-tribally* – then it readily prompts the question of what is so special about tribes. Why not nations, states, even (hideous thought) empires – or at the other end why not provinces, cities, villages, even streets and households? Indeed if the mores of every tribe are as good as those of every other tribe, if it is a kind of epistemological duty so to regard them, why should not one presume that the mores of every individual person are as good as the mores of every other individual? (Not perhaps what every individual actually does but at least what every individual *approves* of doing.) But on second thoughts even this concession may well prove epistemologically unworthy. If nothing is special about what is good or bad, if good or bad are words which

9 William Shakespeare, *King Henry the Fifth*, Act 3, Scene 2, line 116.
10 This is not, of course, to excuse the present and notably odious tribal hierarchy in that country.

always carry with them their own private set of inverted commas, what can be so special about approval? Why should guilt not be seen simply as a form of weakness, a deficit in power? As Thrasymachus saw so clearly – or at least as Plato presents him as seeing – an ethical relativism in politics is linked conceptually to nihilism and nihilism as an ethical doctrine makes it impossible for an agent to have good reason to deny to himself anything which he desires and which he is able to appropriate.[11] The rational man is the psychopath, negotiating obstructions to his desires with instrumental panache – and any internal inhibition in ensuring the way of his future desire is merely a personal or social superstition. A species whose habitat is a world of self-righteous nations or tribes or villages is a species of rational psychopaths whose rationality is impaired solely by their shared or private ethical superstitions. This is not an altogether attractive vision; but if human selves were in truth nothing more than bundles or collections of different perceptions (as David Hume put it)[12] there is perhaps no very pressing reason why it should not be judged as simply a true vision.

Nationalism, then, is simply one level in a conceptual continuum which reaches from the single morally irresponsible individual to the morally irresponsible species man the whole globe over – man, an intelligent being no longer conscious of a dependence on any being higher than himself and left to decide what ends to act for, all on his own – man become, as John Locke put it, 'a god to himself'.[13] Nationalism is simply one version of the self-righteous politics of ethical relativism. But it is certainly at present the version best sustained by political realities, the most causally effective version of this politics at any point on the continuum between the individual egoist and the self-righteously appropriative species.[14] The prevalence of nationalism is a moral scandal because the official ethical culture of almost the entire

11 Plato, *Republic*, ed. Cornford (359D), pp. 43–45. For a clear account of Plato's argument at this point see Terence Irwin, *Plato's Moral Theory: The Early and Middle Dialogues*, Oxford 1977, pp. 186–7.
12 David Hume, *A Treatise of Human Nature*, (Bk 1, Pt 4, Section vi), Everyman ed. London 1911, Vol. I, p. 239.
13 See above chapter 2 note 27.
14 For recent arguments directed against this self-righteousness at the level of the species see Peter Singer, *Animal Liberation*, pb. ed. London 1977 and Stephen R. L. Clark, *The Moral Status of Animals*, Oxford 1977. And for an admirably sane response to such thoughts, more firmly committed to the species, see John Passmore, *Man's Responsibility for Nature: Ecological Problems and Western Traditions*, pb. ed. London 1974.

world is a universalist ethical culture. But, moral scandal though it be, its efficacy is unmistakable. If democracy is the resolved mystery of all constitutions, nationalism is perhaps the resolved mystery of all *boundaries* in a world which is densely practically related across boundaries – a world of international exchange and drastically unequal power and enjoyment. An appropriate symbol of the intuitive economic nationalism of modern populations is the extreme suspicion with which multi-national capitalist corporations have recently come to be held – agencies which are not merely practically beyond the control of sovereign states, politically unresponsible, as internal institutions like armed forces may often prove in practice to be, but which are, because of their mode of organization, in effect constitutionally responsible to no agency at all for how they operate as a whole. There is no state today so ramshackle that it cannot muster an ideological proclamation of why its citizens should trust it. But multinational corporations *have* no plausible ideology of why anyone should trust them. All they can offer is the obvious truth that they trade as they can on the markets, as they find them (and *trade* should not be read in any narrowly legal sense). It is unlikely in fact that there are any multinational corporations as intensely undeserving of human trust by those whom they affect as a fair number of states today. But even a true paragon amongst them, a multinational corporation *sans peur et sans reproche*, could not muster the ideological resources of the most barbarous of states.

Why should this be so?

Nations in the world today are in the first instance not as the word still suggests, extended ideological glosses on kinship units, communities of birth. Rather they are simply states which are relatively happy with their statehood, states in which whatever other features of the social arrangements are widely felt to require amendment, at least no very large grouping within the population feels urgently that they would be much better off in two or more state units, in place of a single one. In this sense the nationhood of most states in the world today is potentially in jeopardy and the nationhood of not a few – including for example Great Britain and Canada – is plainly in jeopardy in actuality. But for our purposes at this point what matters is not simply that today somewhat more nation-states have their national status actively in question than would have been the case three decades ago, but rather what is more or less universally seen as the appropriate replacement for the nationally-jeopardized state – namely the constitution of a plurality of states whose title to nationhood would be comparatively (at least for a time) beyond dispute. The rationality of this process of fission within allocative units to produce what are felt to be more trustworthy communities of common interest is not confined, of course, to nation states. It can be seen at work as transparently and at least as actively within the process of state fission within the Nigerian Federation as it can within the politics of the British Isles. The search for a more intuitively plausible scale of community lies behind the worldwide pressures for decentralization and localization of political choice and control. The search for more locally advantageous distributive arrangements by the same token is a natural consequence of any at all participant political process. Since virtually all political distribution is zero-sum in character[15] in the present tense, whatever its longer term consequences for all the parties concerned, there are bound at any time where distribution is actually occurring to be those who can clearly and accurately perceive themselves as losers and perceive others as winners. Those who are suffering discrimination, other things being equal, have the best of reasons for preferring to exercise the choices themselves. Of course other things never are equal – the present being in terms of political evaluation so much the least significant of political tenses. But illusory though its rewards may eventually prove, the present remains an amazingly powerful locus of political causation; and delayed gratification remains a singularly unenticing political programme. The strains on states, the growing pressures towards fission, can thus be expected to increase for the present, and the only forces which are at all likely in practice, at least in the reasonably near future, to diminish them would be a decrease in effective political articulation and participation, an increase in autocratic control either from the right or from the left. The Soviet Union certainly does have less difficulty with its nationality question than the United Kingdom. This was hardly what one would have predicted late in 1917[16] and it is plain enough that the main agency which has produced the difference is not the superior equity of the Soviet arrangements but rather, to steal a phrase from a recent British Tory prime minister in a rather different context, 'the smack of firm government'.

15 For a helpful introduction to the theory of zero-sum games see Anatol Rapoport, *Fights, Games and Debates*, Michigan 1960, caps. 6–9. (The concept of the zero-sum is introduced in cap. 7) For the Prisoner's Dilemma game and the ways in which (by altering the rules) it is possible to improve upon the outcome, see caps. 10–13.

16 E. H. Carr, *The Bolshevik Revolution*, Vol. 1, London 1950, Part III, 'Dispersal and Reunion'; and Richard Pipes, *The Formation of the Soviet Union: Communism and Nationalism 1917–1923*, 2nd ed. Cambridge, Mass. 1964.

Nationalism

But if nationhood is now revealed in this fashion as the political Achilles heel of many modern states, it remains true that the vehicle in which the whole population of the world formally accepts its common species unity is a Union of *Nations* (or in its earlier version a League of Nations). Even at its most ideologically pretentious the species has not yet *conceived* a practical form in which to transcend the nation-state.

Late twentieth century political organization is the product of a geopolitical process, a process which has followed the constitution of a world market and which is in the broadest and most nebulous of terms a product of the dynamic of capitalist development. Now that this geopolitical and economic field has been constituted, has come into existence, the two broadly alternative ideological orientations towards its existence both implicitly recognize its centrality in modern political choice. Either to embrace the world market and the far from narrowly economic terms of trade which it brings with it, in accordance with classical liberal foreign trade ideology and the doctrine of comparative advantage, or to reject the world market and embrace some version of autarky as an exit from the imperialist noose,[17] 'Economic Nationalism Within One Country', is to see the nation as the key unit of political choice. The bold options for autarky or for an open economy, and all the more cowardly or prudent intermediary stages between these points which are what most nations opt for in fact, can only be and must be exercised at the level of the nation. Twentieth century geopolitics is still conducted predominantly at the level of the nation state and nation states (obviously of very unequal power) are its official dramatis personae. If you do not happen to like your nation state, the plain alternative at the political (if not at the individual) level is to make a new one. If you do not like India, try Pakistan. If you do not like Pakistan, try Bangladesh. If you do not like Nigeria, try Biafra. If you do not like Canada, try *Québec Libre*. If you do not like Britain, try Scotland. If you do not like Scotland, try, perhaps, the Shetlands.

Since twentieth century nation states are in this sense communities of fate and not of choice, since despite Locke[18] one is everywhere today

17 See e.g. Samir Amin, *Unequal Development: An Essay on the Social Formations of Peripheral Capitalism*, tr. B. Pearce, Hassocks, Sussex 1976 (p. 383: 'The transition, envisaged on a world scale, must start with the liberation of the periphery. The latter is compelled to have in mind, from the beginning, an initial local mode of accumulation.').

18 John Locke, *Two Treatises of Government*, ed. Peter Laslett, 2nd ed. Cambridge 1967, II, para. 117, ll. 8–13: '*thus the Consent of Free-men, born under Government, which only*

born a citizen of a particular state unless one has the transcendent misfortune to be born a citizen of no state at all, and since nation states are, as we noted earlier, for the most part democratic in their own conception of their legitimacy (nervously eager, at least at the ideological level, to ingratiate themselves with their own populations as a whole, or at a minimum, to portray themselves as truly representing the latter), and since nation states today are both organizationally and in terms of social process so much more participant societies in terms of literacy, media, physical communications and public expression than any territorial states of the past, one can see readily enough the complicity between state powers and subject populations in determining the locus of the interests which these powers should represent.

Nationalism is the natural political sentiment for modern states and (although many items of nationalist sentiment may be morally pernicious and many others may reflect a dramatic level of false consciousness) there is a solid core of nationalist sentiment which is no more morally discreditable and no more inherently an indication of cognitive confusion than Bentham's principle of self-preference.[19]

If we ourselves are not for us, who else is likely to be?

But if nationalism is in some sense the natural political sentiment for the populaces of modern states and if its predominance in modern politics is thus nothing at which to be surprised, it has certainly not been at all a natural sentiment for most human beings in most of human history, nor even for the great majority of the populations of very large states at least until well into the twentieth century. The

makes them Members of it, being given separately in their turns, as each comes to be of Age, and not in a multitude together; People take no notice of it, and thinking it not done at all, or not necessary, conclude they are naturally Subjects as they are men'. Locke did not, of course, intend to deny the legal fact that, according to English law, the status of subject is indeed acquired at birth. But he had the greatest difficulty in reconciling this fact with his theory of political obligation (see John Dunn, 'Consent in the Political Theory of John Locke', *The Historical Journal*, X, 2, June 1967, pp. 153–82).

19 For an extreme presentation of the implications of this principle, see Bentham's 1822 account of the publication of the *Fragment on Government:* 'Now, for some years past, all inconsistencies, all surprises, have vanished: everything that has served to make the field of politics a labyrinth, has vanished. A clue to the interior of the labyrinth has been found: it is the principle of self-preference. Man, from the very constitution of his nature, prefers his own happiness to that of all other sensitive beings put together: but for this self-preference, the species could not have had existence. Place the chief care of each man in any other breast or breasts than his own (the case of infancy and other cases of intrinsic helplessness excepted), a few years, not to say a few months or weeks, would suffice to sweep the whole species from the earth' *(The Works of Jeremy Bentham*, ed. John Bowring, Vol. X, Edinburgh 1843, p. 80). When writing less histrionically, Bentham readily acknowledged that the happiness of nice persons includes a concern for the happiness of at least *some* others.

situation of a Chinese peasant before the mid nineteenth century was one to which peoples outside the empire were essentially (with the exception of a few Mongol forays) almost wholly irrelevant. The Chinese certainly looked down on foreigners,[20] those Chinese at any rate who had heard of the existence of foreigners. (One should remember that as late as 1936 when the nationalist students of Peiping and Tientsin went to the people in the approved Russian style to alert the Chinese peasantry to the threat of Japanese aggression in Manchuria, most of the peasants although they had heard vaguely of Japan, the homeland of the Eastern Dwarfs, had never heard of Manchuria, the nearest point of which was a mere hundred miles away.)[21] If the Chinese did indeed corporately look down on foreigners, the mandarins discharged this burden on behalf of Chinese society as a whole, along with all the other agreeable perquisites of their office. Cultural chauvinism is a common enough motif in history but on the whole until relatively modern times cultural chauvinism has been an elite prerogative – a pleasure for those with the leisure to savour it. Most peoples in history have had their cultural chauvinism done *for* them.

Any society by and large prefers its customs to those of other societies. Indeed to possess customs which one prefers to those of others is what from a cultural point of view it is to *be* a society. Any society is likely to fight, if the need arises and if it feels there to be any chance of success in so doing, for the ashes of its fathers and the altars of its gods.

Nor is chauvinism, where it exists, necessarily a defensive psychological adaptation. English popular chauvinism clearly existed to be appealed to in the audience for whom Shakespeare wrote *Henry V*; and, more urgently, it formed a major emotional theme in the English protestant self-understanding as this can be seen developing from Foxe's *Book of Martyrs*,[22] through the exploits of Sir Francis Drake and Queen Elizabeth's speech to her people at Tilbury[23] to the foreign policy of Cromwell[24] and the Glorious Revolution of 1688. When John

20 John K. Fairbank (ed.), *The Chinese World Order*, Cambridge, Mass. 1968.
21 John Israel, *Student Nationalism in China 1927–37*, Stanford, Calif. 1966, p. 136.
22 William Haller, *Foxe's Book of Martyrs and the Elect Nation*, London 1963.
23 For this speech, delivered on 9 August 1588, in anticipation of Spanish invasion, see J. E. Neale, *Queen Elizabeth I*, pb. ed. Harmondsworth 1960, p. 302. For an interesting discussion of the forces behind the formation of this orientation see Carol Z. Weiner, 'The Beleaguered Isle. A Study of Elizabethan and Early Jacobean Anti-Catholicism', *Past and Present*, LI, May 1971, pp. 27–62.
24 For a brief account see Christopher Hill, *God's Englishman: Oliver Cromwell and the English Revolution*, pb. ed. Harmondsworth 1972, pp. 148–61.

Locke was packing his books to go into exile after the crushing of the Exclusion movement and the temporary triumph of Stuart absolutism, he tacitly titled the manuscript of his Whig tract the *Two Treatises of Government*, (or so Peter Laslett has conjectured),[25] *De Morbo Gallico* – on the French disease – the fetchingly chauvinist English medical name for venereal disease. The conjecture itself is perhaps overbold since Locke was in fact a doctor and possessed a number of medical texts on the topic in question. But if the conjecture itself may well not be true, it is certainly *ben trovato*. Absolutism was seen by many English thinkers in the late seventeenth and early eighteenth centuries as a filthy continental affliction and English or as it became British constitutional liberty were seen complacently as the natural political felicity of a naturally healthy people. British protestant constitutional liberty was the ideological core of a political community in contrast to continental European and often papist absolutist slavery throughout the period that English domination of the world economy was being generated. Here again an ideology of popular representation, a more participant economy and a deeper emotional allegiance to the state power go very closely together. If nationalism is the resolved mystery of all boundaries, one can see readily enough why the English (along with their slightly earlier commercial rivals and Protestant coadjutors the Dutch) should have been the first to resolve the mysteries.

The articulation of this type of chauvinism is connected fairly directly to warfare. The great dates of national chauvinism are almost all either dates of battles or dates of peace treaties which conclude successful wars of national liberation – Bouvines, Bannockburn, Agincourt, the Spanish Armada, Valmy, the Battle of Britain. War has been the great motor of nationalist expansion, not simply in the mechanically important sense of territorial extension by military conquest – what made Spain and Italy and Germany and China and India and Russia into the nations they now are – but also in the more elusive but psychologically at least equally significant sense of constituting national solidarity. The nineteenth century French thinker Ernest Renan answered his 1882 query 'What *is* a nation?', with the memorable phrase 'a daily plebiscite'[26] – that is, a continuous exercise of

25 See Locke, *Two Treatises of Government*, ed. Laslett, 2nd ed., pp. 62–4.
26 Ernest Renan, *Qu'est-ce qu'une nation?*, Lecture given at the Sorbonne 11 March 1882, 2nd ed. Paris 1882, p. 27. 'Une nation est donc une grande solidarité, constituée par le sentiment des sacrifices qu'on a faits et de ceux qu'on est disposé à faire encore. Elle suppose un passé; elle se résume pourtant dans le présent par un fait tangible: le

popular consensual will. This is hardly a causally very adequate vision of the determinants of nationality but it does point to the centrality of will and commitment within the realities of nationhood. We have no reason today to acknowledge the existence of circumstances in which it would necessarily be agreeable to die for one's *patria*; but in any realistically imaginable political world there will remain circumstances in which it would still be, as Horace put it, decorous to do so. Within the present nation-state system states remain compulsive communities of minimal security, machines for human self-defence. And self-defence at a communal level, the defence of ways of living, rights, collective autonomies, cannot be an individualist matter, cannot be morally or practically discharged by individual egoism. 'I love my country [*la patria mia*] more than my soul', said Machiavelli in a splendidly and characteristically histrionic phrase.[27] To choose to obey the universal requirements of Christian ethics, rather than to respond to the practical contingencies of communal defence, was a selfish and a communally irresponsible choice – within nature as it was and plainly would remain, it was a morally *wicked* option, however sanctimoniously and however sincerely rationalized. Christianity was the mortal foe of citizenship, encouraging a sickly concern for the health of the individual soul at the expense of the most pressing requirements of mutual practical responsibility. Nature precludes the normative universalism of moral absolutes, Christian or indeed secular. Machiavelli would certainly have regarded a secular pacifism in a militarily threatened country as being as improper an elevation of individual spiritual self-regard over the practically given duties of the citizen's station as he would a pacifism or Kantian dedication to truth-telling founded on Christian belief. Machiavelli, one may say, simply took consequentialism seriously from a moral point of view.

But it is probably more immediately revealing to note simply that he took the duties of citizenship or republican statecraft, the priority of right of community over individual, as axiomatic, as classical political

consentement, le désir clairement exprime de continuer la vie commune. L'existence d'une nation est (pardonnez-moi cette métaphore) un plébiscite de tous les jours, comme l'existence de l'individu est une affirmation perpétuelle de la vie.'

27 See Machiavelli's letter to Francesco Vettori, 16 April 1527, some two months before his death: 'amo la patria mia più dell'anima' (*Lettere*, 321: Niccolo Machiavelli, *Tutte le Opere*, ed. M. Martelli, Florence 1971, p. 1250); and cf. his praise in the *Florentine History* (Bk III, 7: in Martelli (ed.), *op. cit.*, p. 696) of the Florentine leadership during the city's war with Pope Gregory XI in 1375–78: 'tanto quelli cittadini stimavano più la patria che l'anima'.

theorists had done more effortlessly before the Christianization of Europe.[28] As Hegel observed three centuries later hussars with shining sabres could teach men their public obligations,[29] could bring these home to them in a way in which daily life in peacetime could hardly be expected to do – eliciting a due moral commitment to a context of mutual relations which individuals are normally in a position to afford to treat in a detached and instrumental fashion. In recent European experience the hussars with shining sabres have taken the guise of SS armies, the Gestapo or the military and police agencies of Panzer communism. The experience, above all, of the European resistance in the course of the Second World War stands as a commanding reminder of the political obligation to lay down one's life for one's friends.

It is because of this stark conceptual boundary to the politics of egoistic self-preservation that the ties between membership of a moral community, the duty to defend such a community and the resonance of nationalism as a political ideology are so intimate. It is hard to exaggerate the significance of the link between nationally-predicated political sentiment and the military defence or liberation of what remain today national political communities. The process of national liberation is a process which has done much to form nations. It has not been simply a mechanical external protection of existing cultural and social units but rather a mode in which communities of cultural and social interaction have come to be created. To see the process externally is readily to see it as a process of rather threadbare ideological fiction, supplemented by coercion and murder, the American view of the role of the NLF in South Vietnam.[30] But hussars with shining sabres have a lengthy ancestry. It was largely the Duke of Alba's imperial forces which made the United Netherlands into a nation. It was as much as anything else Napoleon, the agent of an imperialism rationalized in universal terms, that gave some real political substance to German

28 The absurdity of Christian political ethics, the core of Machiavelli's *negative* political doctrine, is a central theme of both *The Prince* and *The Discourses*. But it is the *Discourses* and not *The Prince* which contains his positive political doctrine of the public good. For a penetrating account of his theory in its historical context see Quentin Skinner, *The Foundations of Modern Political Thought*, Cambridge 1978, Vol. 1, pp. 117–38, 153–86.

29 G. W. F. Hegel, *The Philosophy of Right*, tr. T. M. Knox, Oxford 1942, Addition to para. 324, pp. 295–6. For a valuable discussion of Hegel's understanding of the political meaning of war see Shlomo Avineri, *Hegel's Theory of the Modern State*, Cambridge 1972, pp. 194–207, esp. 195–200.

30 For an especially clear picture of this kind see e.g. Douglas Pike, *Viet Cong: The Organization and Techniques of the National Liberation Front of South Vietnam*, Cambridge, Mass. 1966.

nationalism.[31] And the same causal strand can be followed readily enough throughout European colonial expansion and its revanchement – Ireland, Latin America, China, India, Vietnam, Indonesia, Algeria, Guiné Bissau, Kenya, Angola, Cambodia – perhaps in the future even Israel and South Africa. Plainly one should not sentimentalize this process. The birthpangs of nations or even their rebirths are often hideous affairs, years or decades drenched in blood. Think of Cambodia.[32] And history frequently leaves precipitates of problems which are beyond any morally plausible political solution – like the City of Belfast today, a historical absurdity of more than three hundred years depth, attempting to live amidst the ruins of three centuries of history.

Our political sensibilities in advanced industrial societies shy away from these histrionic issues. We think of politics in terms of production and distribution – as an allocation problem – and where violence enters our horizons at all at a level more complex than that of our safety in walking the streets it does so more or less at the level of the unthinkable, a world war fought with nuclear weapons: *Götterdämmerung*. Those of us who are anxious about such matters express our anxieties, with varying degrees of hysteria or plangency. But even for the most anxious it is hardly a matter with much bearing on everyday life. Either it will happen or it won't. Most believe it won't. You or I perhaps, some persons at any rate, believe it will. Some of those who believe it will, feel the need to bear witness to their expectations in as conspicuous a way as they can devise. But even the most spectacular witness can hardly with sanity be expected to have much *effect* on the probabilities of its occurring or not occurring. Either it will happen or it won't. For private citizens at any rate (if not for advisers of American presidents or Soviet party secretaries) a high degree of fatalism seems *à propos*. And so blood and death and the community of unhesitating sacrifice appear to us to be nothing properly to do with politics, atavistic survivals within our own politics, bombs in London or Birmingham, kidnappings and murders in Quebec, or palpable indices that the politics of others in distant places – Chile, Argentina, Italy even, the Philippines, Cambodia – remain the politics of savages, pre-political, pre-civilized, barbarous. And thus the nationalism of tariff barriers or indigenization

31 See note 35 below.
32 François Ponchaud, *Cambodia Year Zero*, tr. N. Amphoux, pb. ed. Harmondsworth 1978, is in places a trifle naive. But it explains why authoritative information on what has occurred is necessarily unavailable and provides convincing grounds for supposing that much which has occurred has been atrocious.

of employment appears as simply a component of modern political reason and the nationalism of those as yet unable to erect tariff barriers and the violence which disfigures this seems archaic and irrational, irredeemably morally ugly. Now it is certainly an error to hint, let alone to *argue*, that these values are simply misconceived – that civic peace and prosperity are not real political goods and goods self-evidently to be preferred to cheery mutual maiming and torture, let alone the hecatombs of slaughter required for (or at least incurred in) the liberation of some nations. But what must be emphasized very firmly is that the comfortable political vision of distributive politics as exhausting the political meaning of membership in a community is an extremely callow and superficial one. And if nationalism as a political force is in some ways a reactionary and irrationalist sentiment in the modern world, its insistence on the moral claims of the community upon its members and its emphasis that civic order and peace is not a given but an achievement which may well have to be struggled for again is in many ways a less superstitious political vision than the intuitive political consciousness of most capitalist democracies today.

It is in this sense broadly true that the populations of most if not all capitalist democracies today espouse a relaxed and peaceful economic nationalism but shrink back rather from the stridencies and the violence of those whose nations still appear to them to require liberation, to be still *unfree*. And it is natural for them thus to see the former versions of nationalism as harmless and the latter as purely damaging, fit conduct for Palestinians. Yet both of these more or less reflex judgements are disastrously inadequate. The relaxed economic nationalism of operating states, although it is a natural outcome of the dynamics of the world economy, poses a real threat to the future of the species, while the terrorist politics of national liberation, unprepossessing though it certainly is in itself, is premised upon very deep truths about the human political condition which it is wildly imprudent for us to ignore.

The perils of economic nationalism are simple enough in outline. To treat economic cooperation in a rigorously zero-sum mood,[33] seeking permanently and at whatever external cost to others to minimize one's own losses and to maximize one's own gains, may be an ecologically viable practice in the short term. But it is a blatantly wasteful way in which to utilize the resources of the globe and the pretence that it does not diminish the natural inheritance of the species, does not violate

33 See note 15 above.

what Professor Macpherson christened Locke's 'sufficiency limi-tation',[34] is palpably absurd. As a practice, it simply does not leave as much or as good in common to other men in the present, let alone in the future. But the deficiencies of such egoistic utilitarian conscious-ness, both imaginative and moral, are not in any sense peculiar to nationalism. They display themselves as conspicuously in the domes-tic politics of advanced industrial capitalist societies as they do in the international postures of all states in the world today.

The distinctive splendours and menaces of nationalism as such come out much more drastically in the relation between individual and community. In exploring the ramifications of this theme it would be hard to exaggerate the centrality of Germany, a culture without a state, as the nineteenth century dawned, confronting an all-too effective state endowed with a universalist ideology. The late Professor Plamenatz has drawn a persuasive distinction between two political forms of nationalism in modern history.[35] On the one hand he sees a

34 C. B. Macpherson, *The Political Theory of Possessive Individualism*, Oxford 1962, pp. 211–14. Locke, *Two Treatises of Government*, ed. Laslett, II, paras. 33, 34, 41 and 43, pp. 309, 314–16.

35 John Plamenatz, 'Two Types of Nationalism', in Eugene Kamenka (ed.), *Nationalism; the Nature and Evolution of an Idea*, pb. ed. London 1976, pp. 22–36. The role of Germany in the development of the intellectual appreciation of the significance of human cultural particularity and in the genesis of modern nationalist political theory can be investigated from a number of vantage points. The most striking of these remains the great trilogy of Freidrich Meinecke: *Cosmopolitanism and the National State* (1907), tr. Robert R. Kimber, Princeton 1970; *Machiavellism: the Doctrine of Raison d'État and its Place in Modern History* (1924), tr. D. Scott, London 1957; *Historism: the Rise of a New Historical Outlook* (1936), tr. J. E. Anderson, London 1972. (See also his slightly earlier and much briefer sketch *The Age of German Liberation, 1795–1815*, tr. P. Paret & H. Fischer, Berkeley, Calif. 1977. For Meinecke's own development see Robert A. Pois, *Friedrich Meinecke and German Politics in the Twentieth Century*, Berkeley, Calif. 1972.) The German intellectual context of the eighteenth century is treated in exceptionally illuminating fashion by Peter Hanns Reill, *The German Enlightenment and the Rise of Historicism*, Berkeley, Calif. 1975 and over a considerably longer span of time by Leonard Krieger, *The German Idea of Freedom: History of a Political Tradition*, pb. ed. Chicago 1972. Klaus Epstein, *The Genesis of German Conservatism*, pb. ed. Prince-ton N.J. 1975 is a monumental study, relating the social and political background of different areas of Germany to the changing intellectual culture in an impressive fashion. For the Prussian experience in particular see Henri Brunschwig, *Enlighten-ment and Romanticism in Eighteenth-Century Prussia*, tr. F. Jellinek, pb. ed. Chicago 1974; Hans Rosenberg, *Bureaucracy, Aristocracy and Autocracy: the Prussian Experience 1660–1815*, pb. ed. Boston 1966; Walter M. Simon, *The Failure of the Prussian Reform Movement 1807–1819*, Ithaca, N.Y. 1955; Peter Paret, *Yorck and the Era of Prussian Reform 1807–1815*, Princeton, N.J. 1966; Peter Paret, *Clausewitz and the State*, Oxford 1976. For an interesting study of a less militarily dynamic area in the eigh-teenth century, see T. C. W. Blanning, *Reform and Revolution in Mainz, 1743–1803*, Cambridge 1974. For the development of political theory more specifically, see Reinhold Aris, *History of Political Thought in Germany 1789 to 1815*, London 1936;

form, for which Germany is clearly prototypical, in which ethnic and linguistic groups which in terms of culture and civilization are clearly the equals if not the superiors of the polities which rule over them set themselves to forge independent political units of their own as the natural political expression of existing cultural and social capabilities. On the other he sees a form for which a good many of the states of tropical Africa would serve as very adequate prototypes, in which social groupings are in the simplest descriptive sense backward, largely preliterate, with low productivity, weak overarching social solidarities and slight abilities to organize themselves for the better. Nationalism in these territories was a relatively powerful and unambiguous sentiment in the face of colonial rule but it has proved quite intolerably undirective in practice in the aftermath of independence and even in ideological terms has the greatest difficulty in transcending the level of rather brutal self-parody. The passage from *négritude*, a Parisian intellectual conceit, through for example Zambian humanism to the stage in which in Zaïre, the former Belgian Congo, authenticity has come to be defined in terms of President Mobutu's proudly wearing the skins of endangered species is not an inspiriting cultural efflorescence.[36] But it is perhaps an adequate enough tracer at the cultural level of the degree of political and social progress over the time-span in question.

In its early nineteenth century German context, from Herder to Fichte or Savigny for example, nationalism did become an explicit ideology of cultural particularism, a sturdy defense of the virtues of the Teutonic folkways in contrast with the brittle polish of Gallic cosmopolitanism, and alongside this a more intractably conservative affirmation of the merits of treating law as a practical expression of historical social continuity, a means for a community happy with itself to guarantee its own reproduction through time, as opposed to the Enlightenment image of the law as instrument of social invention and

Herbert Marcuse, *Reason and Revolution: Hegel and the Rise of Social Theory*, 2nd ed. New York 1954; George Armstrong Kelly, *Idealism, Politics and History: Sources of Hegelian Thought*, Cambridge 1969. Studies which focus more directly upon the impact of the revolution and of Napoleon include Robert R. Palmer, *The Age of the Democratic Revolution: A Political History of Europe and America 1760–1800*, Vol. 2, Princeton 1964, cap. XIV, pp. 425–58; Jacques Droz, *L'Allemagne et la Révolution française*, Paris 1949; Jacques Droz, *Le Romantisme allemand et l'état: résistance et collaboration dans l'Allemagne napoléonienne*, Paris 1966. (See also his *Le Romantisme politique en Allemagne*, Paris 1963).

36 For two versions of the earlier portion of this historical trajectory see Imanuel Geiss, *The Pan-African Movement*, tr. Ann Keep, London 1974 and Robert W. July, *The Origins of Modern African Thought*, London 1968.

rationalization and appropriate field for the exercise of moral creativity.[37] Some of this movement of thought and feeling was, as Hegel for example proclaimed as resonantly as Marx did,[38] simply superstitious and irrationalist. But it was not this more or less effective ideological reinforcement to the practical conservation of social and political arrangements which would have been much better abandoned which has given to nationalism in politics such an appropriately filthy name. What achieved this consequence was the acquisition by these culturally self-defensive and self-protective communities of an altogether too effective single state of their own. Cultural nationalism at home, practised between consenting adults in national privacy or bravely if somewhat furtively devised within someone else's imperial domain, was a harmless and in many ways an edifying business. But cultural nationalism abroad, as the impetus behind a potential conquest state, an ideology of self-righteous and externally irresponsible force was to leave such innocent imaginative gropings far behind. What *it* led to directly enough was the drive for *Lebensraum*, for cultural self-protection and for the physical space in which to practise such assertion to the full. And, when eked out with the more historically adventitious ingredient of racism it led on beyond the early inspirations of the Fascist regimes of Mussolini and Hitler to the charnel house insanity of the Final Solution.[39] This indubitably *was* something new under

37 See above note 35.
38 Two interesting texts of Hegel on specifically German political topics are available in English in Z. A. Pelczynski (ed.), *Hegel's Political Writings*, tr. T. M. Knox, Oxford 1964, pp. 143–294. (For a characteristic comment see p. 282: 'One might say of the Wurtemberg Estates what has been said of the returned French *émigrés*: they have forgotten nothing and learnt nothing. They seem to have slept through the last twenty-five years, possibly the richest that world history has had, and for us the most instructive, because it is to them that our world and our ideas belong. There could hardly have been a more frightful pestle for pulverizing false concepts of law and prejudices about political constitutions than the tribunal of these twenty-five years, but these Estates have emerged from it unscathed and unaltered.' For a useful discussion of this orientation of Hegel's thinking see Shlomo Avineri, *Hegel's Theory of the Modern State*, 34–80, 181–3. For the intensity of Marx's reactions see particularly his early articles, Karl Marx & Frederick Engels, *Collected Works*, Vol. I, London 1975, pp. 109–376.
39 Most of the attempts to trace the cultural roots of national socialism (or, more broadly, of fascism) have not been intellectually very convincing. For a variety of perspectives on the German and Italian regimes themselves Joachim C. Fest, *Hitler*, tr. R. & C. Winston, pb. ed. Harmondsworth 1977; Alan Bullock, *Hitler: A Study in Tyranny*, pb. ed. Harmondsworth 1962; J. P. Stern, *Hitler: the Führer and the People*, pb. ed. London 1975; Franz Neumann, *Behemoth: The Structure and Practice of National Socialism*, London 1942; Karl Dietrich Bracher, *The German Dictatorship: the Origins, Structure and Effects of National Socialism*, tr. Jean Steinberg, pb. ed. Harmondsworth 1973; Adrian Lyttleton, *The Seizure of Power: Fascism in Italy 1919–1929*, London 1973; F. W. Deakin,

the sun. In comparison with this even the ideologies of past, of present and one must blindly hope of future imperialist rule are sensitive, humane and balanced. The cheery acceptance of the Roman destiny to rule the peoples of the world, graciously sparing the vanquished and casting down the pretensions of any people who were haughty enough not to recognize this destiny, the more moralized complacencies of the French *mission civilisatrice*, lineal descendant of the universalism of 1789, or even the ideology of the Russian empire today, shiftier in its practical application but at least more edifying within its own explicit terms, all of these had or have their disfigurements. But none of them can hold a candle to the Third Reich. Since this is what modern nationalism, the nationalism of politicized folkways within the modern capitalist state *did* at one time lead to, it is scarcely surprising that we should view the relationship between cultural nationalism and the modern state with anxiety and suspicion.

It is important, of course, not to be too expansive with one's suspicions. We must separate as sharply as we can the question of what went wrong in Germany, a dense and firmly causal question about society, economy and polity over a particular span of time, from the question of what went wrong in cultural nationalism, what fundamental ideological flaw within cultural nationalism as a set of values the German experience of 1933–45 did in fact disclose. There is an easy universalist answer which simply claims that there was never anything much right about nationalism, that any ideology of cultural self-protection was simply intrinsically reactionary and that is all there is or was to say about it. But this answer is so easy as not to be an answer at all. Indeed it is little more insightful or illuminating as a political judgement than the judgement that if the entire human race had been controlled in its conduct throughout its history by a profound understanding and acceptance of the Sermon on the Mount, most of the horrors of this history as it has in fact occurred would have been avoided. So indeed one might expect.

To see nationalism as being *simply* a bad thing is both politically shallow and morally – at least in part – mistaken. For cultural nationalism is in the first instance little more than the valuing of existing human

The Brutal Friendship: Mussolini, Hitler and the Fall of Italian Fascism and The Last Days of Mussolini, pb. eds. Harmondsworth 1966. For a broader perspective see Ernst Nolte, Three Faces of Fascism, tr. Leila Vennewitz, pb. ed. New York 1969. Nicos Poulantzas, Fascism and Dictatorship: the Third International and the Problem of Fascism, tr. Judith White, London 1974 is a Marxist treatment, raising important questions but failing to provide convincing answers to these.

social identity at a point in time when this has come to feel itself under pressure. It is not necessarily culturally bigoted – committed to the infliction of its own local cultural proclivities in a hegemonic fashion on the rest of the world. Indeed, as Isaiah Berlin has eloquently insisted,[40] the first great protagonist of cultural nationalism, the German social philosopher Herder, took the view that it was *necessarily* opposed to any such venture. Valuing the plurality of cultures and languages, the subtle ecological variety and nuance of human practices, distinctly for themselves, for their existent idiosyncracy, rather than assessing their merits in terms of their conformity with or deviation from some supposedly humanly universal aesthetic or ethic, he refused to see hierarchy within the realm of cultures and insisted that, as structures of lived sentiment, they must instead be accorded intrinsic value rather than appraised sternly from the bastion of a single culture. Herder's thought was not especially rigorous. But he was, as far as we know, the first thinker to see at all clearly the very intimate and profound implications of the fact that man is above all else an animal that uses an extremely elaborated language and to sense the profound political implications which the extent of (and the limitations on) practical inter-communication between human languages must present. Because both what man makes himself and a large part of what he is caused to become are mediated by human speech, the potential community of those with whom men can in practice communicate, to whom they can in practice render themselves lucidly intelligible, can be a human community in an altogether deeper sense than practical aggregations of human beings of any scale who are unable to address each other or comprehend each other with such directness. To understand a human being as a human being is to understand him as an actual or potential speaker, in terms of what, if speaking honestly and with due attention, he would have to say. This is an extremely banal point and it has been very extensively ventilated by recent social theorists, though unfortunately largely in German and by theorists who clearly experience some difficulty in making themselves lucidly intelligible even in that formidable tongue.[41] For the moment all we need note in this context is the dependence on such potential intelligi-

40 Isaiah Berlin, *Vico and Herder: Two Studies in the History of Ideas*, London 1976, pp. 157–63, 194–5.
41 See particularly the works of Jürgen Habermas, *Theory and Practice*, tr. J. Viertel, pb. ed. London 1974 and *Knowledge and Human Interests*, tr. J. J. Shapiro, pb. ed. London 1972; and of Hans-Georg Gadamer; *Truth and Method*, tr. G. Barden & J. Cumming, London 1975 and *Philosophical Hermeneutics*, tr. & ed. David E. Linge, pb. ed. Berke-

bility of the possibility of real human commitment to one another, not simply as in Christian interpretations of universalist natural law as members of a biological species with obligations to preserve ourselves and other members of the species – but real commitment to one another as we actually are, highly elaborated and self-interpreted cultural creatures. Herder, it seems, sensed this when he wrote, with a scorn a little reminiscent of Edmund Burke's[42] that 'The savage who loves himself, his wife and his child . . . and works for the good of his tribe as for his own . . . is in my view more genuine than that human ghost, the . . . citizen of the world, who, burning with love for all his fellow ghosts, loves a chimera. The savage in his hut has room for any stranger. . . . The saturated heart of the idle cosmopolitan is a home for no one.'[43]

Since we are all in some measure, in the age of television and air travel, cosmopolitans in ghostly communion, we must hope that Herder is wrong. And certainly when the political consequences of nationalism are considered on a world scale, as they plainly should be, it would be more than foolish to see its main consequence as the preservation of the bonds of social affection and its main beneficiaries as those who feel such affection most keenly. If we are all also in some measure nationalists now we are scarcely such because we have all come to care for one another more.

So let us remember once again why it is that we *are* all nationalists now and ask in conclusion what perils are associated with this condition.

ley, Calif. 1977. For a helpful introduction to the work of Habermas see Richard J. Bernstein, *The Restructuring of Social and Political Theory*, Oxford 1976, Part IV, 'The Critical Theory of Society'; and Anthony Giddens, 'Review Essay: Habermas's Social and Political Theory', *American Journal of Sociology*, LXXXIII, 1, July 1977, pp. 198–212 and 'Habermas's Critique of Hermeneutics' in Giddens, *Studies in Social and Political Theory*, London 1977, pp. 135–64. For a more flat-footed Anglo-Saxon conception of the implications of such a viewpoint see John Dunn, 'Practising History and Social Science on Realist Assumptions' in Christopher Hookway & Philip Pettit (eds.), *Action and Interpretation*, Cambridge 1978, pp. 145–75.

42 Edmund Burke, *Reflections on the Revolution in France*, Everyman ed. London 1910, p. 44: 'To be attached to the subdivision, to love the little platoon we belong to in society, is the first principle (the germ as it were) of public affections. It is the first link in the series by which we proceed towards a love to our country, and to mankind. The interest of that portion of social arrangement is a trust in the hands of all those who compose it.'

43 Herder, *Ideas for a Philosophy of the History of Mankind* (Bk VIII, 5), quoted in Berlin's translation from Isaiah Berlin, *Vico and Herder*, p. 178. For a translation of the greater part of the section of the text from which this is drawn see J. G. *Herder on Social and Political Culture*, (ed.) F. M. Barnard, Cambridge 1969, pp. 307–11.

Nationalism

We are all nationalists now, *analytically*, because Marx's analytical universality – the insistence that modern social, economic and political process must be seen as a totality at the level of the globe – has worn so much better than the political universality of his proletarians has done.[44] It was a misfortune perhaps – a nasty historical accident, a malign jest of *Fortuna*, that Socialism should have had to start off so firmly within one country – though one may in retrospect see all too plainly that Socialism was necessarily prone to this type of accident. But it was in any case always a necessity that Socialism would have to begin within particular countries, with particular boundaries, controlled by particular powers. And in the long run it is hard to see how any set of boundaries could fail in some measure to resolve its mystery.

Within particular countries, however their polity is organized, it will continue to make sense for their inhabitants to define common interests and to will (and even to attempt to cause) their governments to protect these to the best of their abilities. The rational and moral core of nationalism in an all too practically integrated world is the protection within boundaries of local cultural and economic and political interests. The immoral (and sometimes, though not always, irrational) penumbra of nationalism is the attempt to enforce such interests to the direct damage of those of others.

The key question for the rationality of nationalism is the question of how far in such an integrated world it is correct for the inhabitants of different territories to see their interests, cultural, economic or political, in zero-sum terms, as matters in which the gain of one is necessarily the loss of another. There is really no surviving tradition of thought which provides at all a plausible method of answering this question with any confidence or generality, though in different ways, liberal international trade theory and Marxist political rhetoric both pretend brazenly from time to time to be able to do so.

And the stumbling bemused idiom of thought which looks most realistic in its insistence on the idiocy of defining all interests in zero-sum terms – that deep terror that we may be systematically destroying in the pursuit of our several short-term interests the global ecology which offers our only habitat – *this* idiom has no boundaries to teach us its realities in modern daily life (because its only boundary is the globe itself) and controls no governments, compelled to enforce its definition of our common interests. If it does now constitute the conventional

44 Karl Marx & Frederick Engels, *The German Ideology* (1845–46), *Collected Works*, Vol. V, London 1976, pp. 48–54.

wisdom of the species as a whole, it is a conventional wisdom without a trace of political power at its disposal.

For human interests at the level that modern nationalism rationally articulates them within boundaries, modern history has duly created nation-states to defend them in some fashion. But for those more final interests which stretch across all boundaries and on which the very survival of the human species (and vast numbers of other species along with it) arguably now depends, modern history has not so far been thoughtful enough to supply agencies with the least capability of defending them. It is easy to parody Marx's slogan with an appropriate modern analogue. 'Human beings of the world unite, you have nothing to keep but your habitat.' But as to telling us how to set about the project and how we could expect to be successful at it, that, alas, is quite a different thing.

4

Revolution?

'I am not yet so lost in lexicography, as to forget that *words are the daughters of earth, and that things are the sons of heaven*.'

    Samuel Johnson, *A Dictionary of the English Language*, Preface, 1755. (The original is unpaginated. The complete Preface is reprinted in E. L. McAdam Jr & George Milne (eds.), *Johnson's Dictionary: A Modern Selection*, London 1963).

'Do not stop half way and do not ever go backward. There is no way behind you.'

    Mao Tse-Tung, 21 June 1967 (quoted from Frederic Wakeman Jr, *History and Will*, pb.ed. Berkeley, Calif. 1975, p. 275).

'Il le faut avouer, le *mal* est sur la terre.'

    Voltaire, December 1755. (*Poème sur le désastre de Lisbonne ou examen de cet axiome: tout est bien*, line 126: *Oeuvres Complètes de Voltaire*, ed. Louis Moland, Vol. IX, Paris 1877, p. 474).

What has been claimed thus far is that democratic theory is the unthinking normative political theory of the modern West and that liberalism is its painfully precarious reflective normative theory. What makes liberalism such a painfully precarious *political* theory, we have suggested, is the obtrusive chasm which separates it from the world, as it is and as it very much still seems to be becoming. In this sense nationalism is simply a comforting if shifty accommodation to the practicalities. What we need to consider in conclusion is whether, as hinted at the end of the previous chapter, accommodating to the practicalities in this particular disposition may not in the end prevent the practicalities from holding up – may not simply in the longer term prevent the possibility of morally civilized social and political life *continuing* on earth. And, if it may and even *does* imperil the human future in this way we need further to consider whether there is any sound reason for hoping or expecting that it can in fact be changed for the better. For if the world can with any confidence be altered for the better, there are probably few human beings, other things being equal, who would fail to choose, in the spirit of Marx's eleventh thesis on Feuerbach,[1] to change it rather than simply to interpret it.

If a drastic change in the terms of mutual human social relationships is certainly a great deal for which to hope, it may still in practice prove over time to be the least change in relation to which the emotion which we would have good grounds for feeling would be *hope* at all: once again, as Rosa Luxemburg warned, socialism *or* barbarism.[2] But one can only coherently *hope* for, wish devoutly for, consummations which one can coherently conceive. Is there an honestly imaginable *possible* future for the species for which it would be morally sane to hope and even, according to one's abilities, to struggle? There are certainly well-argued pragmatic capitalist scenarios for the world as a whole which envisage a future of increasing economic prosperity, at least for those who are already economically prosperous or who subsequently prove to have been blessed by geography. How far such projections are overoptimistic even within their own somewhat blinkered terms is a severely technical question and one on which only economists possess the technical capacity even to reflect at all seriously, let alone to pronounce with assurance in public. But what one can be certain of, even without such skills, is how very narrow these terms are and how grossly they fall short of any morally coherent vision of the interests of the species as a whole. There simply *is* no plausible capitalist vision of a morally possible future for human beings even in the most flatly

1 Karl Marx, *Theses on Feuerbach*, Marx & Engels, *Collected Works*, Vol. V, London 1976, p. 5: 'The philosophers have only interpreted the world in various ways; the point is to *change* it.' This text differs slightly from that published by Engels as an appendix to his *Ludwig Feuerbach and the End of Classical German Philosophy*.

2 'Friedrich Engels once said "Capitalist society faces a dilemma, either an advance to socialism or a reversion to barbarism." What does a "reversion to barbarism" mean at the present stage of European civilization? We have read and repeated these words thoughtlessly without a conception of their terrible import. At this moment one glance about us will show us what a reversion to barbarism in capitalist society means. *This world war* means a reversion to barbarism. The triumph of imperialism leads to the destruction of culture, sporadically during a modern war, and forever, if the period of world wars which has just begun is allowed to take its damnable course to the last ultimate consequence. Thus we stand today, as Friedrich Engels prophesied more than a generation ago, before the awful proposition: Either the triumph of imperialism and the destruction of all culture, and, as in ancient Rome, depopulation, desolation, degeneration, a vast cemetery; or, the victory of socialism, that is, the conscious struggle of the international proletariat against imperialism. Against its methods, against war', Rosa Luxemburg, *The Junius Pamphlet: The Crisis in the German Social Democracy, February–April 1917*, quoted from Rosa Luxemburg, *The Mass Strike*, pb. ed. New York 1971, p. 111 & see also p. 216. For analysis of Luxemburg's thought see especially J. P. Nettl, *Rosa Luxemburg*, 2 vols, London 1966 and Norman Geras, *The Legacy of Rosa Luxemburg*, London 1976.

utilitarian of terms, each counting for one and none for more than one – just as there can be no morally approbatory vision of the existing world order which is not based on a pronounced degree of moral astigmatism or myopia. It is well known that socialism also has more than a little difficulty in keeping a very happy moral face on its present. But, unlike capitalism, it has never hesitated in its efforts to unite theory with practice, to draw heavy drafts on the future.

It has least difficulty in so doing, of course, where it has slightest practical effect. As an idiom of pure moral intention it can readily be as edifying as one could wish. But since it is officially committed to scorning pure moral intention, this will be slight consolation. And even as an idiom of pure moral intention considerable doubt has been cast on its success in avoiding prevarication and even incoherence.[3] The effortless synthesis of moral individual and moral community, of easy freedom and intense responsibility, which one finds most eloquently expressed in some of the earlier works of Marx looks on close inspection exceedingly like an intellectual confidence trick. This is of some practical importance, of course, since if as Leszek Kolakowski for instance argues,[4] Marxism has never in fact made sense, it is scarcely surprising that history should have failed so dismally to realise its hopes and its promises. But in itself this line of thought is perhaps not especially illuminating. However important the possible equivocations at the heart of its moral and social theory may be in cementing the affections and credulities of those who espouse it as a militant faith, it does not seem likely that the impact for better and for worse of Marxism upon nineteenth and more especially twentieth century history has been much controlled by the fundamental conceptual properties of its moral theory.[5] These are, to be sure, of great significance to political philosophers. But historians and political scientists have themselves often been more than a little credulous in the extent to which they have seen these conceptual properties operating as causal

---

3 See e.g. Leszek Kolakowski & Stuart Hampshire (eds.), *The Socialist Idea: a Reappraisal*, London 1974, especially chapters 1 & 2 by Kolakowski himself. While it is plainly not the author's intention to licence such an inference, it would not be difficult for the pessimistic to arrive at similar conclusions on the basis of reading Perry Anderson, *Considerations on Western Marxism*, London 1976.

4 See Kolakowski, 'The Myth of Human Self-Identity: Unity of Civil and Political Society in Socialist Thought', in Kolakowski & Hampshire (eds.), *op. cit.*, pp. 18–35.

5 Although its scholarship is now in some areas a little dated, the best survey of the historical influences to which Marxism as a political doctrine has been subjected remains the late George Lichtheim's splendid *Marxism: An Historical and Critical Study*, London 1961.

forces in revolutionary and post-revolutionary political action. As a revolutionary theory Marxist socialism in a number of varieties has certainly had a drastic effect on the political history of the twentieth century; and if the effect has been somewhat different from that initially hoped for and advertised, there is always the future to be called in to redress the balance of the present. Marxists today, of course an extravagantly wide spectrum of opinion – almost as wide as Christians – but still recognizably a single spectrum, can see the relevance of their self-understanding to the riddle of history today – its partial or complete solution[6] – in terms of some balance or other between the abstract extremity of their initial moral promise and the morally less appetizing but practically startling impact of what their fellow Marxists have caused to occur, at least since 1917. At the very minimum, as a continuing language spoken by huge numbers of people in a wide variety of places, Marxist socialism continues to promise, by more or less ingenious or ingenuous equivocation between its moral aspirations and its practical consequences, a practical future for the species as a whole which is at least *presented* as a fully moral future. Some of all this is certainly just a matter of force and fraud. But we do need to ask with urgency whether all of it is no better than force and fraud, whether socialism in the face of man's place in history today is simply the political name for the practice of agreeable self-deception. The word above all others which bridges the gap between all too finite practical consequence and virtually infinite but as yet unrealized promise is the word 'revolution'. Revolution is both the name of sundry more or less profoundly esteemed past historical episodes – in France, in Russia, in China, in Vietnam, in Cuba[7] – and also the name of the transcendently different future of a rescued world, a world rescued from the traumas of capitalism and thus rendered truly human at last.

6 Cf. the initial expectations: Communism 'is the *genuine* resolution of the conflict between man and nature and between man and man – the true resolution of the strife between existence and essence, between objectification and self-confirmation, between freedom and necessity, between the individual and the species. Communism is the riddle of history solved, and it knows itself to be that solution', Karl Marx, *Economic and Philosophical Manuscripts* (1844), Marx & Engels, *Collected Works*, Vol. 3 London 1975, pp. 296–7. And see Marx & Engels, *The German Ideology* (1845–46), *Collected Works*, Vol. 5, pp. 48–54, esp. p. 49: 'Communism is for us not a *state of affairs* which is to be established, an *ideal* to which reality (will) have to adjust itself. We call communism the *real* movement which abolishes the present state of things.'

7 For a somewhat crudely nominalist emphasis on the heterogeneity of twentieth century revolutions see John Dunn, *Modern Revolutions: an introduction to the analysis of a political phenomenon*, pb. ed. Cambridge 1972. For a very proper structural corrective see Theda Skocpol, *States and Social Revolutions in France, Russia and China*, Cambridge 1979.

Marxism, it may well be thought, sees quite deeply into these episodes and into the history from which they have emerged and from which as a species we do indeed require with growing urgency to engineer our rescue. But its vision of how the rescue is to be secured is altogether too dishonest to be prudent and too imprudent to be wholly sane – trading as it does on primitive fantasies of the extirpation of evil and cultivating a mood of spite and paranoia. If there is to be any prospect whatever of the species coming to share the globe in decent amity and fellowship with another, a more eirenic and less morally self-entranced consciousness will certainly be one of its necessary conditions. Optimistic Marxists at any rate are in this measure right enough as to what is so deeply wrong with the world and as to what has brought this wound about. But they are just grotesquely wrong in their callow confidence as to what can reasonably be expected to bring it all to rights, to heal it. Where, then, does this confident and wildly misconceived understanding come from?

The history of the understanding of revolutions, the disintegration of regimes under their own internal strains and the convulsive restructuring of society and polity in the wake of this disintegration, is extraordinarily complex and, as yet, very poorly understood. This is not a context in which it would be appropriate to attempt to explore it at all seriously. But it is necessary to say a very little, cursorily and recklessly, about the place of the idea of revolution in the political theory of Karl Marx himself. When Marx was a relatively young man, before the year 1848, his conception of the *political* character of revolution was largely dominated by the great French Revolution, the history of which he studied at considerable length.[8] After the failure of the 1848 revolutions and after his statement to the September 1850 Meeting of the Central Committee of the Communist League[9] Marx turned his attention increasingly away from the importunities of practical revolutionary action towards political work of an appreciably slower rhythm and towards a more and more profound attempt to grasp the logic of the process of global economic change which he had already

8 For Marx's early theoretical understanding of revolution see Michael Löwy, *La théorie de la révolution chez le jeune Marx*, Paris 1970; Jean Bruhat, 'La Révolution française et la formation de la pensée de Marx', *Annales Historiques de la Révolution Française*, XXX- VIII, 184, April–June 1966, pp. 125–70; R. N. Hunt, *The Political Ideas of Marx and Engels*, Vol. 1, London 1975. Bruhat is particularly helpful on the impact of the French example. Marx at one point worked for some time on the project of writing a history of the Convention.
9 See chapter 2 note 12 above.

long decided to be the fulcrum of the history of the modern world and which the history of the world ever since has increasingly confirmed to be indeed such. There are some interpretations of this shift which seek especially to emphasize the increasing moral sobriety and fastidiousness of the politics of the older Marx, its relatively effortless mutation towards the politics of social democracy,[10] while there are others, more politically wedded to the heritage of Lenin, and leaning heavily on Marx's fierce solidarity with the Commune of 1871[11] and his more opportunistic invoking of insurrectionary ventures within the Russian empire,[12] which wish to insist on the strict continuity between the permanent revolution of early 1850 and the Bolshevik venture of October 1917.[13] The hermeneutics of texts as sacred and as practically consequential as these is bound to be as intricate as it is inflammatory and it is, accordingly, 'no accident' that there exists not one single study of the development (or stasis) of Marx's thinking about these questions the conclusions of which one could remotely trust.[14] But it seems on balance plain enough that both of the main traditions of interpretation, the Social Democrat and the Leninist, are at present decidedly straining interpretative licence on the issue. The Leninists palpably exaggerate Marx's expectation of the causal contribution

10 See especially George Lichtheim, *Marxism: An Historical and Critical Study* and *A Short History of Socialism*, pb. ed. New York 1970.

11 See Karl Marx, *The Civil War in France* (1871), Marx & Engels, *Selected Works*, 2 vols, Moscow 1958, Vol. 1, pp. 473–545. For correctives to this interpretation see Henry Collins and Chimen Abramsky, *Karl Marx and the British Labour Movement: Years of the First International*, London 1965, Parts IV & V, and Shlomo Avineri, *The Social and Political Thought of Karl Marx*, pb. ed. Cambridge 1970, pp. 185–201, 239–49.

12 See especially A. Walicki, *The Controversy over Capitalism. Studies in the Social Philosophy of the Russian Populists*, Oxford 1969, esp. pp. 179–94; and Baruch Knei-Paz, *The Social and Political Thought of Leon Trotsky*, Oxford 1978, Appendix, pp. 585–98.

13 See e.g. Neil Harding, *Lenin's Political Thought*, Vol. 1, *Theory and Practice in the Democratic Revolution*, pb. ed. London 1977, esp. pp. 105, 114–15. (Harding's careful and interesting study presents a convincing view of the development of Lenin's thought; but it is distinctly less authoritative in the implicit view which it offers of Marx's own conception of political action and the appropriate division of labour between intellectuals and proletarians within this.) Robin Blackburn (ed.), *Revolution and Class Struggle: a reader in Marxist politics*, pb. ed. London 1977, especially the contributions by the editor and Ernest Mandel, pp. 9–135; Georg Lukács, *Lenin: A Study on the Unity of his Thought*, tr. N. Jacobs, pb. ed. London 1972 (a study which in practice serves well enough to underline the extent of the gap between the politics of Lenin and those of Marx).

14 This is not to say that there has not been a considerable volume of interesting writing in the last decade on the interpretation of Marx's politics. See, for example, Ralph Miliband, *Marxism and Politics*, London 1977; R. N. Hunt, *Political Ideas of Marx and Engels*; Hal Draper, *Karl Marx's Theory of Revolution. Part I. State and Bureaucracy*, 2 vols., New York 1977.

which centrally orchestrated terror and repression would have to make to the engineering of the post-revolutionary Communist order and because they do so, in their historically very proper desire to emphasize Marx's fierce commitment to the reality and earnestness of political struggle, his intractable bluntness and distaste for moral ornament and discretion, they also greatly exaggerate his sheer zest for violence and repression and the consequent degree of sympathy which can plausibly be imputed to him for political action which will result and *has* now resulted in the construction of highly effective and durable-looking tyrannies. It might of course be the case that the regrettable disappointment of the hopes of the younger Marx amounted to nothing more consequential than just that, the failure to eventuate of a contingently overoptimistic prediction. But if Marxist theory is to be taken seriously at all, as, having changed so much of the world so drastically, it can scarcely fail to claim as its entitlement, such consistently overoptimistic predictions surely deserve closer attention and it becomes appropriate to inquire whether the theory itself does not somehow secrete inherently overoptimistic predictions.

There are by now overwhelming grounds for believing that it *does* indeed do so. Marx's deepest insight was his conception of capitalist production as a systematic process for specifying human goals in mutual conflict and one in which in consequence the social and political units within which production was to be organized were necessarily and permanently structurally vulnerable. It is clear enough by now that when Marx first came to formulate this conception he saw it in a misguidedly teleological fashion – as an indication that this form of society must necessarily proceed and proceed in some haste towards a *terminus ad quem* of a different social form which was free from such structural contradictions. Not only did he at first perceive it in this over-simply teleological mode, he also drastically misjudged the pace of its progress in any distinct direction. In later life he did to some degree come to appreciate this misjudgement and his mature researches in economics were largely motivated by the desire to get intellectually to the bottom of it. On balance the best talents which have devoted themselves to the question – even those who continue to work within its idiom – seem now to be agreed that the economic theory which he developed in the effort to fathom these issues was not a tremendous success when it came to doing so.[15] The intellectual

15 The view that Marxist economics as a whole represents an intellectual failure has, naturally, been very adequately ventilated by non-Marxist economists. See, for

limitations of the economic theory itself and the political disappoint-ments of the predictions of capitalist collapse have led many to pre-sume that the initial sociological vision of Marxism has somehow been refuted by the passage of subsequent history. But this seems simply to be a misjudgement. Shorn of its simplistically teleological elements, Marxist analysis is certainly the most powerful theoretical conception of capitalist economy, society and polity and the relations between these which we at present possess (though one should add that to say that it is the most powerful conception which we at present possess is certainly not to say *much*). But of course its simplistically teleological elements remain of crucial importance in politics and most blatantly so when we come to consider the Marxist understanding of revolution.

Marx's own picture of the political promise of revolution at least in advanced capitalist societies remained premised with some firmness on the collapse of the French Ancien Regime in 1789, a structure of social arrangements with its own long-cherished ideology, collapsing beneath the weight of its own sheer ideological implausibility. This was not, of course, Marx's own official conception of the causal dynam-ics of any revolution – that of 1789 certainly included. But since it was such a blatant characteristic of what did actually happen in 1789 (unlike for example in 1793), it was as natural for Marx to extrapolate it from those events as it was for example for Tom Paine to have done so at roughly the time that they occurred.[16] Seeing the political fragility

example, for a particularly haughty dismissal of its residual intellectual significance for economic theory Joseph A. Schumpeter, *History of Economic Analysis*, ed. Elizabeth B. Schumpeter, New York 1954, pp. 883–5. (In a less austerely professional mood Schumpeter took the significance of Marx's conception of the laws of motion of capitalist society extremely seriously: see *Capitalism, Socialism and Democracy*, London 1943.) For a fair appraisal of some of the main weaknesses from committed partici-pants in the tradition see e.g. Anthony Cutler, Barry Hindess, Paul Hirst and Athar Hussain, *Marx's 'Capital' and Capitalism Today*, Vol. I, pb. ed. London 1977, esp pp. 96–101, 157–65, 207–21, 313–28.

16 See especially Karl Marx, *Contribution to the Critique of Hegel's Philosophy of Law: Introduction* (1844), Marx & Engels, *Collected Works*, Vol. 3 London 1975, particularly pp. 184–6 for the parallel (with explicit reference to Sieyès's pamphlet). See also Emmanuel Joseph Sieyès, *What is the Third Estate?*, tr. M. Blondel, London 1963; Thomas Paine, *The Rights of Man, Part I* (1791), Everyman ed. London 1915 p. 104; 'The opinions of men with respect to Government are changing fast in all countries. The Revolutions of America and France have thrown a beam of light over the world which reaches into man. The enormous expense of Governments has provoked people to think, by making them feel; and when once the veil begins to rend, it admits not of repair. Ignorance is of a peculiar nature: and once dispelled, it is impossible to re-establish it. It is not originally a thing of itself, but is only the absence of knowl-edge; and though man may be kept ignorant, he cannot be *made* ignorant.' Paine drew extreme conclusions from this vision: 'Those who talk of a counter-revolution in

of capitalist societies, as he did, so directly in terms of their gross ideological implausibility, their persistently self-regenerating social animosities and their structural liability to recurrent crises of production, it was very easy for Marx to invoke the political action which was to supplant capitalism as prospectively that of the immense majority.[17] When capitalism's night of the 4th of August came round, why should it not prove as hard pressed for ideological defenders as the residual rights of feudalism had been in 1789? An existing form of society, Marx knew as well as Machiavelli or Hobbes, was integrated, preserved, in the last instance by force. But the moral absurdity of capitalist society, brought out more and more blatantly by its own internal dynamics, could be trusted soon enough to deplete the force of those who protected it and to augment the force of those who suffered from it. Seeing political and social crime as secured by force (accurately enough) Marx did not shrink from the exercise of necessary force against it. Revolutionary political action was the action of the socially injured in a just civil war.

All this is fairly standard Marxist apologetic, though not of course expressed in terms with which Marxists would be at all happy. Where does it go wrong? Revolutionary political action, the practice of just civil war, is a precarious attempt (as any putatively just war must be) to synthesize violence and justice. Because of the circumstances in which civil wars are characteristically fought it essays this synthesis in a peculiarly ambitious fashion and on unusually unfavourable terrain, defining the *telos* of revolution, overambitiously, as Utopia and deploying the moral splendour of this intended (or at least proclaimed) destination to excuse what in practice often amounts simply to murder and sometimes to murder on a very large scale. Moreover the reason

France, show how little they understand of man. There does not exist in the compass of language an arrangement of words to express so much as the means of affecting a counter-revolution. The means must be an obliteration of knowledge; and it has never yet been discovered how to make a man *unknow* his knowledge, or *unthink* his thoughts', p. 104. For the speed and decisiveness of the collapse in 1789 see classically Georges Lefebvre, *The Coming of the French Revolution*, tr. R. R. Palmer, pb. ed. New York 1957 and *The Great Fear of 1789: Rural Panic in Revolutionary France*, tr. Joan White, London 1973.

17 Karl Marx, *Manifesto of the Communist Party* (1848), Marx & Engels, *Collected Works*, Vol. VI, London 1976, p. 495. The version quoted is that of the 1888 edition: 'All previous historical movements were movements of minorities, or in the interest of minorities. The proletarian movement is the self-conscious, independent movement of the immense majority, in the interest of the immense majority.' Cf. Lukács, *Lenin*, p. 65: 'The moment of deception lies in *the undialectical concept of the majority*' (Lukács's own emphasis).

why murder on such a large scale so often proves to be necessary (or at any rate proves to be perpetrated) is quite deeply related to the reasons why Utopia fails to eventuate. And the reasons why Utopia fails to eventuate are not, as is usually maintained from within the Marxist defensive perimeter, the Marxist *laager*, that revolutions have not occurred in the appropriate places or at the appropriate times – never the time, the place and the loved one all together – but rather that capitalism – unlike the residues of feudal rights in 1789 – is in fact the way social production actually operates and cannot be supplanted simply by its ideological obsolescence. It can only be *practically* replaced by some other mode of organizing social production. In this matter Marx appears to have fallen a victim to the sort of dialectical illusion which is liable to afflict those with a Hegelian education. Identifying (with some felicity) the transparent moral absurdity of capitalist production, he too readily presumed that the practical conveniences of capitalist production could be appended to a morally less ludicrous manner of organizing production – that a morally rational mode of social production would be relatively effortlessly to hand for those who chose to grasp for it. He never in fact gave any very extensive or any at all plausible reasons for this supposition and by now it seems a reasonable judgement that the reason why he failed to do so is that there *are* no such reasons. The residual ideological plausibility of capitalist society today is a direct product of our collective failure to devise any alternative mode of organizing production which is in practice (as opposed to in theory) ideologically more prepossessing with which to replace it. This may seem a somewhat fanciful judgement in prospering capitalist societies, which are not obliged to press very heavily upon their ideological plausibility. But it is evident enough in those, such as Great Britain, where the residual ideological plausibility of capitalism is virtually all that there is for a government to rely on.

But this ideological precariousness of relatively economically mature (not to say senile) capitalist society has little if anything to do with why revolution has occurred when and where it has thus far done so. Looking at relatively mature capitalist societies today, even at the most mature and ideologically solidary of them all when the lights go out, it is difficult to miss the persisting underlying vulnerability of this form of collective social existence. But casting one's eyes toward the conditions and circumstances of countries which have indeed undergone revolutions it is hard to see any relation whatever between these episodes and the latent promise, purportedly associated with them, of a less morally and practically fragile form of social existence genuinely available within mature capitalist societies. Scanning the twentieth century record to pick out the incidence of revolution the most salient clues to the rationale of this incidence lie in the geopolitical context of national regimes and the intense external shocks to which this context at times subjects them, the vast convulsions of the two World Wars or the pressing diplomatic and military offensives of the greatest world powers – Germany, France, Japan, the United States, the USSR, one after the other, or several at one time. There are no domestic revolutions in the twentieth century, certainly none whose claim to the title of revolution is reasonably uncontentious.[18] And because there are no domestic revolutions there are singularly few revolutions whose political and social meaning is at all adequately characterized as the simple replacement of, supersession of, the power of one class by that of another. The nearest to a counter-example to this claim is the example of the revolution in China, the most intractably, proudly and durably unique of all the great historical societies. Efforts have of course been made, even quite emotionally vigorous efforts, to conceive the Chinese experience as a token of an alternative possible future for industrial capitalist societies. But to see its social and historical meaning as having any such implications for us is to read the auspices with the crazed eyes of faith.

In a transparently just civil war, in which the righteous, the proletariat who can build the new future and can build it finely, confront the unrighteous, the bourgeoisie who can only fight with their backs to the wall to defend an existing order of injustice ever more blatantly at the end of its tether, the moral lines of battle would draw themselves with ease and authority. But since all these lines are so intensely blurred in practice, the self-imputed righteousness of the self-appointed political agents of the proletariat which licenses in their own eyes their fierce incitements to the fracas, wears on the outside too much of an air of entrepreneurial ruthlessness and self-deception to serve as a very commanding title to power in practice. For anyone who shares (as is easy enough to do) most, if not all, of the Marxist picturing of capitalism as a system of practically self-protective and self-perpetuating social injustice, it is thus an especially urgent task to underline the

18 Cf. John Dunn, 'The Success and Failure of Modern Revolutions', in Seweryn Bialer & Sophia Sluzar (eds.), *Radicalism in the Contemporary Age*, Vol. 3, Boulder, Colorado 1977, pp. 83–114; Dunn, *Modern Revolutions; Skocpol, States and Social Revolutions*.

judgement (one which will please scarcely anyone) that what above all has made it possible for these apparently politically self-exposing (free speech – democratic elections etc.) and quite plainly morally exposed societies to go on in the old way is the failure of the political leadership of the new way to show themselves to any great degree deserving of power. On the right, socialist leadership has remained imaginatively and practically imprisoned within the operating rationality of the old capitalist way, aiding rather than imperilling on balance its perpetuation, while on the left socialist leadership has displayed, where it has been of practical consequence at all in mature capitalist societies, an opportunist ruthlessness, a preparedness to gamble gratuitously with the lives of millions, which *prove* it to be unfit for political responsibility. It has failed to win power, because it has failed to seem with any plausibility to deserve power. Where revolutions have occurred in the twentieth century they have done so because the gamble has already been forced upon the populace at large under circumstances in no sense of their own choosing or where the political choice lay between the revolutionary leaders and an incumbent government (as in Cuba)[19] which had proved itself with some rigour and over a very considerable time to be wholly unfit to rule. To choose under any circumstances to gamble with the lives of millions is, to take a phrase from Edmund Burke in one of the most direct and least self-serving sentences of his *Reflections*, 'to play a most desperate game'.[20] To play such a game lightly, even to be eager to play it at all, is by now, whatever it may have been in 1844 or 1848, a morally frivolous taste. Revolutions do sometimes happen when they must, in conditions of acute crisis, when a shape of life has indeed grown old. But to will them out of season and to nurture an easy hatred and a casual callousness to their prospective targets, whole classes or simply political opponents, is a poor recipe for building a better world and a direct enough route to the practice of murder and tyranny. Max Weber's political views were in many ways unattractive;[21] and he was never less ingratiating in their expression than when he came to comment on the brave and doomed leaders of the German Left – 'Liebknecht belongs in the madhouse and Rosa

19 See Dunn, *Modern Revolutions*, cap. VIII; and James O'Connor, *The Origins of Socialism in Cuba*, Ithaca, N. Y. 1970.
20 Edmund Burke, *Reflections on the Revolution in France* (1790), Everyman ed. London 1910, p. 182.
21 For Weber's political views see especially Wolfgang J. Mommsen, *The Age of Bureaucracy: Perspectives on the Political Sociology of Max Weber*, Oxford 1974 and David Beetham, *Max Weber and the Theory of Modern Politics*, London 1974.

Luxemburg in the zoological gardens.'[22] But cruelly put though it was, he did express a profound and dreadful truth, a truth which has rung through the history of the twentieth century like a funeral knell, when he said bleakly of the murder of Liebknecht and Luxemburg: 'Liebknecht called up the street to fight. The street has despatched him.'[23]

The fact that revolutions have occurred then is scarcely in itself reassuring news except for those who both feel the capitalist social world to be irredeemably evil and morally absurd and also expect it, unless violently assaulted head-on, to be likely to succeed in perpetuating itself indefinitely. To those who do indeed share both of these feelings with some intensity the temptation to summon up the streets must be all but irresistible. Of course the streets may ignore the summons and indeed they usually do do so, for better and for worse, for bad reasons and for good. But if in fact there is little reason to expect capitalist societies to be able to perpetuate themselves indefinitely and if we still have dreadfully little idea as to how in practice to build something better to put in their place, then the urge to summon up the street is not merely as so far insisted inhumane and overhasty, imprudent in an egoistic sense, it is also overhasty and imprudent in a profoundly altruistic sense. It imperils directly the collective interests of our species. For what we need, if we are to have the least prospect of learning how to live more decently with one another, either within individual national societies or within the globe as a whole, simply is *not* further practice in learning how to hate one another, more intense and fiercer doctrines of the duty and rationality of mutual odium, yet more grandiose and eloquent (and still equally ill-founded) theologies with which to back our hatreds.

Of course all this is very much easier to say than to translate into categories of possible action, let alone to enact in practice. Remembering Machiavelli we must not mistake it for an anodyne pacifism, the hope that if only we can display our kindness and gentleness with enough eloquence and resonance, the human race might soon be dispensed from the need on occasion to kill one another. Life is real and earnest and we cannot sanely expect in an imaginable future to be able to magic away the right to take human life in defence of threatened

22 Quoted from Anthony Giddens, *Politics and Sociology in the Thought of Max Weber*, pb. ed. London 1972, p. 25.
23 Quoted by Beetham (*Max Weber*, p. 173), from Marianne Weber's life of her husband. The translation of this passage in the English version of this (Marianne Weber, *Max Weber: A Biography*, tr. Harry Zohn, New York 1975, p. 642) differs slightly from Beetham's.

good from among the attributes of political sovereignty. But what we can do is to resist the continuous imaginative tug (to which we are all liable) to see the society of our allegiance, actual or potential, as based, in de Maistre's terrible image,[24] upon the executioner, or to see the political career of struggling to actualize this potential as a vocation of revenge.

But what else is there for us to do towards one another in this increasingly crowded world and at this late and tangled stage of our history but murder one another dutifully and zestfully on one pretext after another, in defence of freedom or socialism or civilization or the revolution? Or, to put the question less hectically, are there still any terms on which, the world and men and the relations between men being taken as they now are, the human species could come to share the world and its resources with one another in security and mutual trust for a lengthy future? To identify such terms with confidence would be to identify how there could be at the global level (and for the first time in human history at any level) a rational political community which could be seen and acknowledged as such, without false belief, by all its members. Nothing less than this can preserve (or, rather, can rescue) the relevance of the tradition of western political theory to the future which we now face. For anything less than this will necessitate the weakening of our commitment to one side or the other of this curious cultural hybrid, with its extremist and uncompromisingly universalist moralism and its equally extremist commitment to understanding nature and man's place in it the way it is – and not some other and more comforting way.

It is this last commitment which is hardest either to satisfy or (deliberately) to abandon. The most exigent of moralisms can be tacitly parochialized with little, if any, intentional effort. The moralization of a national political community, a bounded territorial and demographic unit in a world of other such bounded units, would constitute an impressive moral achievement by the standards of western political reason in the past. (Indeed it would not be a nugatory achievement at present.) But today, even if the moralization were achieved in a non-illusory manner and not merely by the fostering of false beliefs, such a

24 Jack Lively (ed.), *The Works of Joseph de Maistre*, New York 1965, pp. 191–3, esp. 192: 'And yet all grandeur, all power, all subordination rests on the executioner: he is the horror and the bond of human association. Remove this incomprehensible agent from the world, and at that very moment order gives way to chaos, thrones topple, and society disappears. God, who is the author of sovereignty, is the author also of chastisement: he has built our world on these two poles.'

triumph – the construction of a moral island in an amoral ocean – is already morally too little and practically far too late. For the practical community in which we live now is a world community, a community of devastatingly uneven economic development and political division into a bizarre series of feudal apanages. To civilize a single barony within this feudal world – Canada as it might be – or England – is a worthy project in itself. But no one could mistake it for the establishment of a viable moral community.

Around a century and a third ago Karl Marx sketched out for the first time in the manuscript of *The German Ideology*[25] a picture of the creation of the globe as a single frame of action for the human species and hinted gnomically at the possibility of our building a real species community within it. True the actual builders of the community were defined a little hastily as the proletariat, a grouping whom Marx saw as having the superstition gouged out of them by the ineluctable dynamics of capitalist development, a process which would purge the dross from the gold in the developed civilisation and power of the species and leave the proletariat the proud possessors of the gold. Marx's vision (perhaps too concrete a metaphor – Marx's dream at least) of a global species community was drastically rationalist, very much at odds with his sense of the dense facticity of social and economic practices in every actual society. It was a vision in which generosity effortlessly dominated greed and in which neither envy nor fear were allotted any very pressing eventual object. Within particular capitalist societies Marx at first saw civilization and accident-proneness developing, if not side by side, at least in some degree of harmony. Social revolution within particular countries and the building of a fresh frame of social relations between countries were seen as posing no very firm obstacles to each other.

Both of these views, the picture of structural conflict within capitalist societies and the picture of emergent global species community have turned out to be, from Marx's point of view, overoptimistic, especially as to timing. But they have not, even in retrospect, come to look altogether absurd. What has come to look altogether absurd, however, is the view of their relatively effortless compatibility. The motto of all states in the world today, whether covertly or overtly, is 'What I have I hold.' It is imaginatively possible to some degree and probably technologically possible to at least an equal degree for the human species to

25 Karl Marx and Frederick Engels, *The German Ideology* (1845–46), Marx & Engels, *Collected Works*, Vol. V, London 1976, esp. pp. 46–54.

see its position in the world today as a whole and its deepest and most permanent, its *fixed* interests, as held in common. But in political terms the species is organized and organized with enormous rigidity and intractability in a way which obstructs the development of such practical and imaginative community, which defines the interests of classes and of whole societies inflexibly at each other's expense and in the shortest possible run and which backs this definition with overwhelming power. The key problem in practical reason for the species at present is a grandiose and baffling version of the Prisoners' Dilemma;[26] and we can escape it or solve it, if indeed it is still open to us to escape it or solve it at all, only by learning to understand and to communicate more effectively with one another across borders and to muster the imagination to accept broader, more generous and less hopelessly short-term definitions of our interests.

Envy and fear are the psychic forces, the causal pressures, which we can guarantee will be in play in an interdependent world. But unless we contrive to supplement them with sentiments which recognize more generously that we *are* all indeed humans, there will be as little chance of continuing to live together in any sort of practical community as there would have been of maintaining freedom and peace within operating capitalist societies which left the unequal powers of men on the market to determine literally every aspect of human existence, including sheer survival.

We shall, however, hardly come to feel more generously towards one another unless we learn to understand one another a trifle better. It is the history of capitalism, a cruel but creative history, which has made a world in which such understanding – the extension of informed and practical human sympathy throughout the species – is both possible and necessary (practically possible, and morally and practically necessary). But the experience of capitalism has often not been pleasant; and it has also not for the most part been particularly edifying or imaginatively illuminating. The practical world which it has made is for many of its inhabitants a world (as human existence usually has been in the past) of such arbitrary suffering that blind hatred of those responsible for their condition (whoever they might be) is a natural and excusable response. For Cambodian or Burmese peasants or Ghanaian cocoa

26 For the strategic dilemmas of trust, cooperation and threat posed in this game, see Anatol Rapoport, *Fights, Games and Debates*, Michigan 1960, caps. X–XIII; and for a sparer presentation of the essence of it see Brian Barry, *Political Argument*, London 1965, pp. 253–6.

farmers,[27] it is a world too intricate and too inscrutable even to seek to understand; but a world which it is impossible not to resent and blame. To sympathize with such resentments is natural and appropriate, almost as natural and just as appropriate for citizens of the United Kingdom as it would be for the non-peasant populations of the countries concerned. But sympathizing with the feelings does not necessarily imply adopting in its entirety the vision of precisely whom and what to blame.[28] For the mood which this vision of the world tends to evoke is an international equivalent of Blanqui's mildly bovine domestic proclamation: 'What exists is bad. Something else must take its place.'[29] The political outcome of this mood is classically, as it was in Blanqui's own case, more than a little Manichaean. If there is usually some evidential basis for the selection within it of the Forces of Darkness, little more than sheer wish-fulfilment often serves to select what are to be seen as the Forces of Light. We are all in temperament Manichees after a fashion, splitting the good from the bad largely at whim and cleaving to these arbitrary identifications with the fervour of the self-converted. Manichaean politics possess the energy of certitude; but they are also replete with dangers. A narrowly Manichaean vision is inherently casual about causal capabilities and over-focussed on the exercise of moral will. It calls men importunately to stiffen the sinews and summon up the blood, to a struggle to the death.

Such a vision has dogged the intellectual history of the moral rejection of capitalism for well over a century. The rejection of an intolerable present in favour of a predictably safer and better future (and one suspiciously devoid of extended descriptive properties) was politically at the core of the young Marx's passionate hatred for the German society and polity of his day[30] (a hatred transposed with surprising ease onto the more abstract and emotionally distant structures of capitalist production). It was politically at the core, too, of Lenin's epic

27 For the case of Burma, for example, see James C. Scott, *The Moral Economy of the Peasant: Rebellion and Subsistence in Southeast Asia*, New Haven 1976: and for the case of Ghana, see John Dunn & A. F. Robertson, *Dependence and Opportunity: Political Change in Ahafo*, Cambridge 1973 (an instance where the grounds for resentment have increased drastically since the time of writing).

28 Cf. John Dunn (ed.), *West African States: Failure and Promise*, pb. ed. Cambridge 1978, especially the editor's Introduction and Conclusion.

29 Quoted from Alan B. Spitzer, *The Revolutionary Theories of Louis Auguste Blanqui*, New York 1957, p. 135 (a statement made to an interviewer from *The Times*, 27 April 1879).

30 This antipathy is one of the dominant themes of Marx's early writings and figures to some degree in most of them. For particularly vivid examples see the letters from Marx to Ruge, March–September 1843, published in the *Deutsch-Französische Jahrbücher*, Marx and Engels, *Collected Works*, Vol. III, London 1975, pp. 133–45 and

struggle to vanquish the autocracy which had slain his brother and to build a socialist society in its place.[31] More diffusely (and altogether more trivially) it has lain behind the projection onto the peoples of the Third World over the last two decades of the political capacity not merely to transform their own societies for the better but to reverse the distribution of power and wealth in the world as a whole.[32]

One way of characterizing the central flaw in this tradition of political understanding is to see it as lying in a persistent readiness to allow intensity of moral distaste for a present state of affairs to excuse a weakening in the determination to understand (or even to reflect seriously upon) the causal properties of the future social order with which it is hoped to supplant the present. To display such readiness is to allow moral fastidiousness to sanction social credulity; to refuse even to *attempt* to take responsibility for the consequences of one's actions, should these prove to be initially successful. But to identify the flaw in these terms is scarcely to transcend the level of moral abuse. It certainly provides little concrete understanding of why the historical record of socialism in practice should have proved such a disaster. Such understanding is indeed in any case as yet unavailable, since what it requires is nothing less than a causally adequate history of most of the modern world, a facility with which professional historians are as unwilling even to attempt to provide us, as vulgar ideologues (and some types of social scientists) are eager to endow us on the cheap. But perhaps the gist of the explanation of socialism's practical failure can be seen in a union of three considerations: a retrospectively unsurprising but fairly arbitrary historical misfortune, an equivocation in its conception of the creative protagonist of post-capitalist history, and a distinctive original epistemological sin. The historical misfortune is simple enough in outline, however necessarily contentious it may be to see it

Marx's *Contribution to the Critique of Hegel's Philosophy of Law: Introduction* (1844), *Collected Works*, Vol. III, pp. 175–87. There is a helpful treatment of the development of Marx's views in the context of his German environment in David McLellan, *Marx before Marxism*, pb. ed. Harmondsworth 1972.

31 No study of Lenin's intellectual and political life has yet come close to taking the measure of its historical and theoretical significance. One brief work which does a measure of justice to the tragedy involved (both for Lenin himself and for others) and which avoids adopting a posture of undue credulity is Moshe Lewin, *Lenin's Last Struggle*, pb. ed. London 1973.

32 For two symptomatic recent recantations on this score see (at an oecumenical level) Gérard Chaliand, *Revolution in the Third World: Myths and Prospects*, New York 1977 and (more parochially), Claude Rivière, *Guinea: The Mobilization of a People*, tr. V. Thompson & R. Adloff, Ithaca, N. Y. 1977.

as simply a 'misfortune.' Having avoided so successfully the socialist transformation of civilized countries, countries in which socialism *might* have been possible, Western Europe and North America now confront the consequences of the collapse of capitalism in societies in which a socialist civilization, at the stage of development at which it was essayed, was quite certainly impossible. (We do not of course actually *know* that socialism was or is possible anywhere. But we certainly do know, in the wake of this historical misfortune, that there is nothing at all ineluctable in the coming of socialism – that a world-wide barbarism is at least as real a possibility and perhaps an altogether likelier outcome.)

Whether or not socialism is indeed possible, it should also, in the aftermath of this historical mishap, be easier to acknowledge that it has never been overwhelmingly probable. For socialism in Marx's thought (or its fuller consummation, communism) is initially identified not simply as the aftermath of the political, economic and social chaos in which capitalism was fated to collapse, but as the superior system of social relations with which the proletariat could be anticipated to replace this chaos. That capitalism has not collapsed in its heartlands is evident enough, though even its friends now see it as endangered in some of them. But its failure thus far to collapse in this setting has left comparatively unscathed within Marxist political theory the dependable creative capacities of the proletariat. That capitalist society was politically vulnerable was a sound insight, however much the presumed extent of its vulnerability was at first exaggerated. But to suppose that its vulnerability in any sense dictated the genesis of a better form of society was always over-trusting. To presume at any point in history that such a better world was or is securely inscribed in the logic of the past and present has always been insanely optimistic. Marx's own ambivalent vision of the proletariat as historical agent never provided plausible grounds for such optimism. That the helplessly crushed victims of capitalist oppression should contrive to form an effective Fraternity of Revenge[33] was a reasonable expectation, if not in the event a sound prediction. But that they should necessarily contrive out of the resources of such experience to build a better social world was never articulated even as an expectation which deserves to be

33 Cf. Frederick Engels, *The Condition of the Working Class in England* (1845), Marx & Engels, *Collected Works*, Vol. IV, London 1975, pp. 295–583, esp. pp. 581–3; Marx & Engels, *Manifesto of the Communist Party* (1848), *Collected Works*, Vol. VI, London 1976, pp. 477–519.

called reasonable. The best that can be said for such a conception is that it was profoundly democratic in its assumptions, a merit which signally failed to accompany it in its first transit to a society in which the vast majority of the population were in fact peasants.[34] The worst that can be said of it, perhaps, is that it has bestowed on Marxist political theory not merely a facility for, but almost a commitment to, evasion from which it is extraordinarily difficult, even for those who attempt to do so, to escape. Within the theory of the post-revolutionary state, it permits a firm acceptance of both of the contradictory heritages of the French Revolution, the solidarist participatory democracy of the Parisian *sans-culottes* and the centralized repressive and executive capacity of the Jacobin dictatorship, while excusing its exponents from the task of explaining how in practice these can be made to any degree compatible.[35] More abstractly, it licenses the conception of magical moral (and in some cases even pragmatic) potency latent in the practices of proletarian organizations, rendering the category of 'proletarian' a category of *a posteriori* ascription, rather than descriptive social analysis.[36] The resources for evasion which this fluidity of reference affords are so extensive that rational political learning over time and throughout large-scale political groupings or organizations is rendered virtually impossible. Such learning is never easy at the best of times; and Marxists have good reason not to make it any more difficult for themselves than history has already made it for all of us. And if Marxism is indeed *committed* to a belief in such magical powers, such socially necessitated grace, it is important to insist that it is committed to a falsehood.

34 See especially Moshe Lewin, *Russian Peasants and Soviet Power: A Study of Collectivization*, tr. Irene Nove, pb. ed. London 1968 and *Political Undercurrents in Soviet Economic Debates*, pb. ed. London 1975; and Teodor Shanin, *The Awkward Class: Political Sociology of Peasantry in a Developing Society, Russia 1910–1925*, Oxford 1972. The democratic components in Maoism (and much of its indisputable practical value to the Chinese people) are intimately related to its having abandoned in practice at a very early stage the view that the proletariat had either the capacity to make the history of China or any preferential title to enjoy the fruits of the Chinese revolution once this had been made.

35 See Albert Soboul, 'Some Problems of the Revolutionary State, 1789–1796', *Past and Present*, LXV, 1974, pp. 52–74, esp. p. 74: 'The political form of the revolution could only be "at last discovered" when the heavy handicaps of this double revolutionary heritage had been overcome. But does not this double heritage lie in the nature of things, and in the nature of man?'

36 The most acrobatic example of this transposition is provided by the early works of Lukács, *History and Class Consciousness*, tr. R. Livingstone, London 1971 and *Lenin: A Study on the Unity of his Thought*, tr. N. Jacobs, pb. ed. London 1972. For an illuminating picture of the conception involved see George Lichtheim, 'The Concept of Ideology', in his book, *The Concept of Ideology and Other Essays*, pb. ed. New York 1967, pp. 3–46.

Revolution?

If there were good reason to believe that Marxism is a comprehensive and true theory – the science of history invoked for example by Louis Althusser – it would be both impertinent and absurd to seek to persuade its adherents to reconsider any of their commitments. But even Althusser himself disdains the attempt to give reasons for believing it anything of the sort, dilating instead on the epistemological vistas which the presumption of its being such a science would open up.[37] And, if Marxism is instead simply a searching, if only partially achieved, theory of capitalist production, lacking either an adequate political theory of pre- or post-capitalist societies or, still more pressingly, an adequate theory of human nature, persuading its adherents to relax some of their false assumptions is a task of some urgency.

For the situation which we face at present is certainly one which requires for its understanding some real theoretical insight into the relatively determinate properties of capitalist society and of the system of capitalist production on the world scale, if there is to be any prospect of changing these at all decisively for the better. Political and social dispute within the western world[38] still at present constitutes largely a dialogue of the deaf between two traditions of political understanding. One of these conceives capitalist society, validly enough, as a morally threadbare and practically dangerous form of human social organization; but it offers virtually no resources for discussing clearly and honestly the difficulties and possibilities of constructing anything superior with which to replace it. The other refuses to acknowledge, let alone discuss clearly and honestly, the fundamental properties of a world dominated by the capitalist mode of production. The outcome of this dialogue offers little hope of guidance on how it would be rational for us to act in order to stem the spreading moral implausibility of a world which is indeed failing practically (though still comfortable enough in some areas), but confronting an alternative mode of organization which on its present achievements (despite their diversity) can hold moral authority only for the wilfully credulous.

If Marxists are to acquire the capacity to discuss the problems of building a better world in a less liturgically restricted and heuristically obtuse manner they need above all to reconsider their initial epistemic assumptions. Above all, they need to reconsider the supposition that it

37 See, for example, Louis Althusser & Étienne Balibar, *Reading Capital*, tr. B. Brewster, pb. ed. London 1975; and especially the commentary in Susan James, *Holism in Social Theory: The Case of Marxism*, Cambridge University PhD 1978.
38 Roughly the political perimeter within which public dispute of this kind is at all persistently permitted by the holders of state power.

is rational to assail capitalist society in operation without inhibition in the absence of any coherent and experientially-related proposals for a superior form of social organization of production with which to replace it. It is this supposition which is largely responsible for the leaden weight of fideism which, however effectively it may have been extruded from Marxism as an analytic approach,[39] still lies close to the centre of most Marxist understanding of political practice. What enabled Marx in his youth to found this faith[40] was an initial vision of the dynamics of capitalism which saw History as lurching both ineluctably and reassuringly forward. This conception, we can see, palpably overemphasized both the ineluctability and the reassurance inherent in the historical process. It is as impossible now to miss the drastic causal impact of the individual will – Hitler's, Lenin's, Stalin's, Mao's – on the history of the twentieth century as it is to miss the gap between the intended and the actual consequences of the exercise of these more blatantly world-historical wills. If history is neither so ineluctable nor so reassuring as it seemed early in 1848 we plainly need to try to improve our forward vision if we are to have any hope of realizing its better or averting its worse potentialities. Picking a side and stiffening the sinews is certainly an insufficient recipe for rational political conduct.

But from its very beginning Marxism has been profoundly evasive in its attitude to such questions of strategic prudence. (Its exponents have varied, as might be expected, in their tactical sagacity.) Indeed a licence to evade such questions is built into its very theory of human nature which contrives to unite a despondent historicism about the human past with a gratuitously optimistic historicism about the human future. An infinite social plasticity within a sequence of past (and oppressive) social orders is miraculously consummated, with the collapse of capitalism and the eventual construction of communism, in an apotheosis of autonomous mutual charity. Because of the radical

39 As an approach to historical analysis Marxism has never enforced credulity upon its exponents, as the distinguished British tradition of Marxist historiography has made very evident. But it is certainly harder for Marxists (as it is for everyone) to avoid credulity when their analytic work touches more closely on their immediate political aspirations. No one, of course, *intends* to be credulous. For a recent example of the strains at work see the very interesting study by Gwyn A. Williams, *Proletarian Order: Antonio Gramsci, Factory Councils and the Origins of Communism in Italy 1911–1921*, pb. ed. London 1975.

40 He would certainly not himself have been happy for a *faith* to be what it was due to become: cf. the tag which he adopted as his favourite motto, *'de omnibus dubitandum'* (David McLellan, *Karl Marx: His Life and Thought*, pb. ed. London 1973, p. 457).

dependence of human properties on the organization of society which it supposes, the future condition of social organization in the aftermath of the revolution is one in which all present causal understanding of human behaviour may be (or indeed *will* be) superannuated, in which anything not logically contradictory might be true.[41] The imprudence of this view is self-evident. For, if all causal understanding of human nature is superannuated, why should one expect only the more agreeable logical possibilities to be those which are actualized? Why not, rather, presume that the one thing which as human beings we have sound inductive grounds for believing is that, both socially and politically, the future, like the present and the past will be furnished with appropriate grounds and foci for rational anxiety? No social and political theory can be intellectually acceptable in which the properties of human nature are permitted to slip in and out of intelligibility and susceptibility to rational assessment and calculation, just as happens to be dialectically convenient for its exponents. If Marxism is to realize its own original emancipatory vision and to assist us to build a less oppressive social order for particular populations and for the species as a whole, it needs unreservedly to discard this epistemic licence for evasion – to admit its inability to transcend the distressingly myopic and irretrievably anxious capacities for social vision and prevision which human beings share and on which they depend for such secure and amicable cooperation as they can muster.

To see the crucial weaknesses of Marxism in these terms is in part to follow Stuart Hampshire's summons to regard socialism not as a crude political ideology predicated on a fantasy of natural science but as a moral programme corrected or informed by the sciences of man.[42] It is not, however, perhaps fully to adopt the conception which he implies of the extent or indeed the *type* of knowledge which is at present on offer within these last cognitive ventures. Thus far, the sciences of man, extensively practised though they have certainly been in recent decades, have done little more than extend vastly the range of matters over which it is possible for opinion to be moderately well informed. If scientific knowledge is conceived in terms of manipulation and control, it is no doubt correct to presume with Habermas[43] that this is a less than wholly proper goal to which for the sciences of man to restrict

41 Hegelian doubts are at times cast on the applicability of even this constraint.
42 Stuart Hampshire, 'Epilogue', Kolakowski & Hampshire (eds.), *The Socialist Idea*, pp. 247–9 and see also pp. 36–44.
43 See especially Jürgen Habermas, *Knowledge and Human Interests*, tr. J. J. Shapiro, pb. ed. London 1972 and *Toward a Rational Society*, tr. J. J. Shapiro, pb. ed. London 1971.

themselves. But it is also important to recognize that exceedingly little which meets the standards of such knowledge has as yet been produced by the practitioners of the human sciences. It is also at least equally important to recognize that the philosophical guarantees for the availability in practice of such knowledge on which social scientists in recent decades have been inclined to rely – a naively positivist conception of sensory experience as the dictator of unique theoretical understanding, without any conception of the difficulties posed by the inaccessibility of appropriate counterfactuals[44] – are no longer intellectually available in a respectable form.[45] If the construction of socialism does require that its moral and practical programme should be corrected and informed by the sciences of man, it must be acknowledged that in the face of such responsibilities the sciences of man which we at present possess constitute a bathetic failure. To recognize the intrinsic fluidity of the epistemic field of the sciences of man[46] and to recognize the central role of counterfactual analysis, not merely in validating the candidates for explanatory laws within these sciences but also, and at least equally importantly, in characterizing adequately what is humanly the case at a particular time,[47] enforces on us a very different understanding of the character of these sciences from that which at present prevails. It demands that we conceive them as irretrievably moral sciences, cognitive enterprises committed to the necessarily *humble* assessment of social and individual potentiality under extraordinarily refractory conditions, sciences which are not entitled to and which should not expect the protection of professional authority and routinization, but which place awesome demands for sensitivity and moral self-discipline on those who aspire to practise them.[48] It is

44 See especially Alasdair Macintyre, 'Is a Science of Comparative Politics Possible?' in his *Against the Self-Images of the Age*, London 1971, pp. 260–79 and 'Ideology, Social Science and Revolution', *Comparative Politics*, V, 3, April 1973, pp. 321–42.
45 See Mary Hesse, 'Theory and Value in the Social Sciences' in Christopher Hookway & Philip Pettit (eds.), *Action and Interpretation*, Cambridge 1978, pp. 1–16 and Hilary Putnam, *Meaning and the Moral Sciences*, London 1978.
46 See e.g. Philip Pettit, 'Rational Man Theory' and John Dunn, 'Practising History and Social Science on Realist Assumptions' in Hookway & Pettit (eds.), *op. cit.*, pp. 43–63 & 145–75.
47 To analyse counterfactually is to analyse what is the case in the light of what *could*, under other specified circumstances, have been the case. For philosophical analysis see David Lewis, *Counterfactuals*, Oxford 1973 and Ernest Sosa (ed.), *Causation and Conditionals*, pb. ed. London 1975. For the central importance of such analysis in the human sciences, particularly in relation to politics, see Steven Lukes, *Power: A Radical View*, pb. ed. London 1974 and 'Power and Structure' in his *Essays in Social Theory*, pb. ed. London 1977, pp. 3–29; and John Dunn (ed.), *West African States*, pp. 214–16.
48 See Dunn, 'Practising History and Social Science', *op. cit.*, esp. pp. 163–4.

certainly incorrect to presume that either human beings or their practices are in any sense devoid of causal properties. But human sciences which (very appropriately) endeavour to identify such properties must do so with an understanding of how hard it is in principle to know that they have succeeded in doing so correctly. And, because of the modesty which such understanding dictates, and because the objects of such understanding are themselves human beings, singly or in larger masses, such sciences have sound reasons for conceiving themselves in the first instance as sciences of mutual understanding – sciences in the tradition of Socrates and not in the tradition of Newton.

There was never any good reason to believe that a behaviourist science of man would prove much of a success.[49] As King Duncan observes at a peculiarly ironical moment in *Macbeth:* 'There's no art/To find the mind's construction in the face.'[50] But if a science which conceived its human objects simply as extended matter was never a very promising cognitive option, what sort of conception of the objects of their understanding would the more humane sciences of mutual understanding possess? To know the answer to this question at all extensively would be already to know the findings of sciences which scarcely amount as yet to more than intellectual good intentions (when to that). Nor is it easy to be certain of how we should identify the constraints on what could count as valid findings. For to be able to do so would above all be to have identified confidently the appropriate terms of trade between moral respect for human beings (ourselves as much as others) and recognition of their factually given properties. As we have seen already, an essentially liberal conception of human nature as free and responsible agency and a consequent entitlement to respect is at present very poorly equipped to vindicate its claim to secure grounding in the rational comprehension of nature as a whole. Yet alternative conceptions of human nature, more firmly grounded in what purports to be the rational understanding of nature as a whole and more boldly reductive of human metaphysical pretensions, have in no case succeeded in providing coherent grounds for regarding human beings with respect at all.

Standing a little back from these portentous obscurities, it is easy to recognize a practical as well as a theoretical dimension to the possibility

49 For particularly severe criticism of the behaviourist orientation see Macintyre, *Against the Self-Images of the Age* and, in a more general and philosophically elaborated form, Charles Taylor, *The Explanation of Behaviour*, London 1964.
50 William Shakespeare, *Macbeth*, Act I, Scene 4, ll. 12–13.

of valid mutual understanding between human beings. Both the grounds for optimism as to the possibility and the grounds for pessimism as to the probability of such understanding are set out incomparably in Shylock's famous speech:

'Hath not a Jew eyes? Hath not a Jew hands, organs, dimensions, senses, affections, passions, fed with the same food, hurt with the same weapons, subject to the same diseases, healed by the same means, warmed and cooled by the same winter and summer, as a Christian is? If you prick us, do we not bleed? If you tickle us, do we not laugh? If you poison us, do we not die? And if you wrong us, shall we not revenge? If we are like you in the rest, we will resemble you in that . . . The villainy you teach me I will execute; and it shall go hard but I will better the instruction.'[51] To identify another as a responsible human agent may be a necessary condition for according them respect; but it is also a necessary basis for regarding them with resentment.[52] Mutual understanding does not necessarily imply mutual applause. Refusing to recognize the fact of common species membership is indeed irrational:[53] but refusing to acknowledge that it implies any very drastic inhibition of our own desires on behalf of the interests of others is irrational only if we expect them to exercise such drastic inhibition on our behalf. In itself it is entirely rational – merely morally unedifying.

To include ourselves within the same framework of understanding as other persons is a condition of rationality. To cease to set a higher priority on our own interests than that which we set on those of others is a moral achievement. What enables human beings to understand each other (to the degree that they can) is precisely the inclusion of their selves in the same framework as that in which they grasp the condition of others. As Herder put it: 'The degree of depth in our feelings for ourselves conditions the degree of our sympathy with others; for it is only ourselves that we can project into others.'[54] The practical skill which makes such understanding possible is the capacity to use language, a skill which sets the limits both to the possible

51 William Shakespeare, *The Merchant of Venice*, Act III, Scene 1.
52 See, classically, P. F. Strawson, 'Freedom and Resentment', in P. F. Strawson (ed.), *Studies in the Philosophy of Thought and Action*, pb. ed. London 1968, pp. 71–96.
53 For an interesting conflict of views on what this consideration implies see Thomas Nagel, *The Possibility of Altruism*, Oxford 1970 and Gilbert Harman, *The Nature of Morality: An Introduction to Ethics*, pb. ed. New York 1977.
54 Quoted from Friedrich Meinecke, *Historism: The Rise of a New Historical Outlook*, tr. J. E. Anderson, London 1972, p. 315.

privacy of human truth and to its intrinsic determinacy in a fashion which we do not at present at all clearly understand.[55] It is because we can communicate in such an elaborate fashion with one another that we could in principle understand each other well and that we could in principle cooperate together as a species in a manner which did recognize our common species membership more handsomely. But language is only a natural capability. It is left to us to decide to what uses to put it. Nothing compels us to choose to recognize in practice this community of biological fate as the basis for any claims at all on one another. All that can be said is that the natural capacity to understand each other is one which we can, if we so choose, seek to foster culturally and to acknowledge morally.

It is important not to set our sights too high. Mutual understanding entails the possibility of some mutual respect. But it does not entail either the necessity of *any* respect or the possibility of complete respect. (We are all deplorable for some of the time and some of us are deplorable for quite large proportions of it.) It is no use seeking to force ourselves to visit upon others a level and type of respect which we have no good reason to accord ourselves. An appropriate mood for cooperation founded upon a modest level of self-understanding could be more optimistic than that which Hobbes, for example, advocated on this basis,[56] eschewing a morose mutual suspicion, though not com-

---

55 See Christopher Hookway, 'Indeterminacy and Interpretation' in Hookway & Pettit (eds.), *op. cit.*, pp. 17–41; and cf. Dunn, 'Practising History and Social Science', *op. cit.*, pp. 173–5 and Bernard Williams, *Descartes: The Project of Pure Enquiry*, pb. ed. Harmondsworth 1978, pp. 292–303. It is a crucial defect of Marxism as a comprehensive social theory that it can provide no coherent treatment of the nature and significance of this centrally human capability.

56 Thomas Hobbes, *Leviathan*, ed. M. Oakeshott, Oxford 1946. (For the methodological precept see Introduction, p. 6: 'But there is another saying not of late understood, by which they might learn truly to read one another, if they would take the pains; that is, *nosce teipsum, read thyself:* which is not meant, as it is now used, to countenance, either the barbarous state of men in power, towards their inferiors; or to encourage men of low degree, to a saucy behaviour towards their betters; but to teach us, that for the similitude of the thoughts and passions of one man, to the thoughts and passions of another, whosoever looketh into himself, and considereth what he doth, when he does *think, opine, reason, hope, fear,* &c. and upon what grounds; he shall thereby read and know, what are the thoughts and passions of all other men upon the like occasions.' And for the practical precept which Hobbes drew from this, see cap. XIV, p. 92: 'The force of words, being, as I have formerly noted, too weak to hold men to the performance of their covenants; there are in man's nature, but two imaginable helps to strengthen it. And those are either a fear of the consequence of breaking their word; or a glory, or pride in appearing not to need to break it. The latter is a generosity too rarely found to be presumed on, especially in the pursuers of wealth, command, or sensual pleasure; which are the greatest part of mankind. The passion to be reckoned upon, is fear.')

mitting ourselves to a credulous dependence on each other's transcendent nobility.

One view with which such a mood is not, however, readily compatible is the thesis of ethical relativism (the thesis that all societies have the values which they should) – either at the level of whole societies (where it presumes a curious sociological functionalism or secular providentialism) or at a more realistic and differentiated level which merely acknowledges how very diverse, even within any society, human purposes in fact are. As a strictly philosophical thesis ethical relativism is less than plausible either as a contention about the meaning of moral statements or as one about their truth,[57] being dubiously compatible with a recognition of the human capacity to communicate and to resent across cultural frontiers, let alone with a recognition of its urgent practical need to cooperate effectively across them. In more vulgar form (the form in which it might bear upon such practical needs) ethical relativism is either a confused expression of moral respect for other humans as they actually happen to be (or to have been) – in which case its implicit premise contradicts its explicit conclusions – or it is a mere spasm of nervousness, however ideologized, an index of simple infirmity of purpose. That is to say, it is either a misleading way of describing a sentiment which we ought to feel or a psychic debility which fully merits the contempt which history is certain to visit upon it.

But if we cannot escape responsibility for the future which we are making simply by abandoning the practice of moral self-assessment, it is still necessary to consider the question of how it is now rational to seek to make a better future. Is it indeed true that we *could* still make such a future, even if we elected to try to do so? This is in part a theoretical question. Is such a future within the bounds of natural possibility, men and societies being taken as they historically are and as they naturally could be? It is in part also a severely practical question. Even if such a future is indeed naturally accessible from where we now find ourselves, can we collectively muster the determination and the insight to fight our way through to it? The practical question can only be answered in practice. But we are still sadly ill-equipped even to

---

57 On the status of ethical relativism as a philosophical theory see especially Bernard Williams, *Morality: An Introduction*, pb. ed. Harmondsworth 1973, esp. pp. 34–9 and 'The Truth in Relativism', *Proceedings of the Aristotelian Society*, 1975, pp. 215–28; and cf. Gilbert Harman, 'Moral Relativism Defended', *The Philosophical Review*, LXXXVIV, 1975, pp. 3–22 and J. L. Mackie, *Ethics; Inventing Right and Wrong*, pb. ed. Harmondsworth 1977.

address the theoretical question; and we can be quite certain that no one at present *knows* the answer to it. Even if we could more readily agree as to what a juster mode of organizing society on the world scale would consist in, we have at present no means of knowing how far such a just order would be compatible with individual liberty. What we are at present offered the opportunity to choose between are a blind credulity about the compatibility between socialism and freedom on the world scale and a forlorn attempt to present the arbitrary contingencies of capitalist reproduction as an appropriate focus for human moral veneration,[58] a conception which in its blatancy scarcely transcends the provincial vision of Justus Möser in 1790: 'In my opinion, the rights of man consist in the authorisation to take possession of all that is unoccupied and to defend all that has been so acquired.'[59]

Is socialism in fact compatible even with responsible government, with a political order in which the rulers are in practice effectively answerable to those whom they rule? Or is the attempt to combine greater social equality with some real democratization of political authority simply an attempt to violate what Alexis de Tocqueville called 'the ancient laws of society'?[60] No doubt it is true that the ancient laws of society are customarily reiterated theoretically only when they are clearly proving difficult to defend in practice. And it is also instructive to note the increasing expression of doubt as to whether in fact the maintenance of capitalism itself is compatible with even the degree of democracy which we at present enjoy in Great Britain. (Professor Hayek, for example, along with a number of less intellectually consequential figures on the right, is clearly sidling back towards the conclusions reached on the subject by Henry Ireton.)[61] We may also, as noted earlier, be quite certain that we cannot all in fact *rule* our own societies, let alone somehow *rule* collectively the world as a whole. But the extent to which governments can in fact be rendered responsible to those over whom they rule (an extent which, unless it can be increased rather than diminished, will preclude for ever the construction of a

58 See for example F. A. Hayek, *New Studies in Philosophy, Politics, Economics and the History of Ideas*, London 1978 and, somewhat more evasively, Robert Nozick, *Anarchy, State and Utopia*, Oxford 1975.
59 Quoted from Meinecke, *Historism*, p. 285.
60 Alexis de Tocqueville, *Recollections*, tr. A. Texeira de Mattos, pb. ed. New York 1959, p. 116.
61 See, for example, Hayek, *New Studies*, pp. 105–18, 152–62, 304–8 (esp. p. 308) and cf. his letter to *The Times*, 3 August 1978. For Ireton's position see the Putney debates (A. S. P. Woodhouse (ed.), *Puritanism and Liberty*, London 1938, esp. pp. 26–7 & 53–5).

Revolution?

society in any way resembling the aspirations of Marx) is still a very obscure question and one which urgently demands reflection.

The experience of post-revolutionary socialist countries under Marxist auspices cannot be said to show that such democratization, and a consequent extension of freedom, are impossible. But they provide ample grounds for expecting such progress to be extremely difficult to realize.[62] They also make it apparent that the relationship between Marxism as a monopolistic system of belief and a ruling Marxist party which is in a position to exert the rights which it claims to derive from the exercise of a monopoly of moral insight and practical sagacity is, in the absence of effective political restraints, quite appallingly dangerous. Both Marx and Lenin appear to have assumed that socialized production and a very high degree of responsibility of governmental power to society and economy were quite readily compatible.[63] But their reasons for believing this were not well articulated; and the organized political legacy which they have, however unwittingly, left behind them has made their hopes seem more than a little callow. This is not a matter about which it is either forgivable or sensible to be discreet. If Marxist political theory is to learn how to realize its own emancipatory project it needs to develop a quite new level and style of reflection on the question of how in practice and in principle the battle of democracy could be won.

But even the realization in the future of a much fuller level of democratization in socialist society will not magically transform the properties of the *demos*. It is no more possible to presume the *demos* to possess perfect moral taste than it is to presume that their rulers will do so – any more than Marxist theorists should have expected to find it possible over time to sustain the conviction (which they have sometimes expressed) that either the proletariat or the leadership of its party can and will do no wrong. Authority cannot ever reside simply in what any set of human beings contingently happens to decide. Authority,

62 The implications of the Russian experience are analysed in a particularly fair-minded and suggestive fashion in Lewin, *Political Undercurrents in Soviet Economic Debates*. Interesting discussions of the rather different experience of Yugoslavia can be found in Bogdan D. Denitch, *The Legitimation of a Revolution: The Yugoslav Case*, New Haven 1976 and Deborah D. Milenkovitch, *Plan and Market in Yugoslav Economic Thought*, New Haven 1971.

63 See e.g. Karl Marx, *The Civil War in France* (1871), Marx & Engels, *Selected Works*, Moscow 1958, Vol. I, pp. 473–545, esp. 518–24; and *Critique of the Gotha Programme* (1875), Marx & Engels, *Selected Works*, Vol. 2, pp. 13–44, esp. 31–3 & 42. For Lenin see particularly V. I. Lenin, *The State and Revolution* (1917), in V. I. Lenin, *Selected Works*, 2 vols., Moscow 1947, Vol. 2, pp. 141–225, esp. 156–7, 167–75, 177, 180, 201–3, 207–11, 216–21.

109

that is to say, cannot be institutionalized. But, if it cannot, there is some danger in thinking, as social scientists have recently been encouraged to do, of power as the antithesis of authority, the more or less institutionalized capacity to harm the interests of others.[64] Both of the leading ideologies in world politics have been inclined to promise brazenly that power (in this sense) could in some fashion vanish from the world of history. But this is the most abject of deceptions – for the root meaning of power is simply capability, the capacity to act for the better as well as for the worse, for the worse as well as for the better. Power is simply a name in social and political life for human freedom, the capacity to choose what to do. And, if we are none of us quite as free as we sometimes fancy – and if human history is a profoundly resistant medium for individual human action – it is still in fact made by the sum of myriads of individual free actions; and the capacity to act freely is not a burden which we are ever likely to be able to shed. Power will remain in human political and social life because the power to act is central to the destiny of the species, necessary to the way we *have* to live, and because there is no way in principle of rendering it intrinsically harmless. Human beings are free and cognitively fallible agents and because they are both (and perhaps because they are each) they are also morally fallible agents. There can be no structural guarantee of a safe and moral future for the species. We must *make* it together or we must just do without it, create the rational grounds for mutual trust and learn how to sustain them through time – or play, as blithely as we can, amidst the gathering dusk.

The image of such a possibility of rational mutual trust, a shadowy image, but not wholly devoid of shape, can be set out in terms of the somewhat intellectually unfashionable design for political reason expounded in Plato's *Republic*.[65] Plato maintained that the possibility of a good political and social life together depends upon the tautest conceivable relation between power on the one hand, the capacity to determine what social practices do or do not come about, and individual virtue on the other – and he also maintained that individual virtue depends solely and profoundly upon the extent of individual rational insight into the nature of reality, that those who *do* grasp in its full depth the character of the human condition within nature will always act, simply under the compulsion of their own degree of understanding, for the true good of their fellows. This is not to say that their

64 See particularly Lukes, *Power: A Radical View*.
65 *The Republic of Plato*, tr. Francis M. Cornford, Oxford 1941.

emotions will become dominated by a sloppy, shallow and complais-
ant benevolence, an inability to disapprove what other men shabbily
feel or still more shabbily enact at one another's expense. It is simply to
say that those who do indeed know and understand, the philosopher
rulers, will, by sheer force of their understanding, be purged of the
animal passions of self and transformed into obedient instruments of
the demands of reason and the good. Rational understanding, in this
perspective, and especially rational understanding in relation to questions of practice, of what is to be done and how men should live, has as
its logical prerequisite or its necessary causal consequence (or some
heady package of the two), the establishment of a secure hegemony
of reason over the passions. To invert Hume,[66] in such men,
philosophers, men fit to rule, the good, the passions are and ought to
be and can be only the slaves of Reason. In Plato, this doctrine,
notoriously enough, is used to sanction the most defiantly elitist of
political conclusions, conclusions which are so deeply at odds with the
pieties and shibboleths of contemporary political culture the world
over, and, more importantly, at first sight so distressingly complacent
in their presentation of the social location of moral dependability that it
requires a considerable effort of will for us today to consider them at all
seriously. But although they certainly are distastefully elitist and based
in part on biological beliefs of Plato's which (although their contemporary descendants do not lack for adherents) are quite preposterously
false, they are also in some respects at least appreciably more honest
and realistic than what passes for moral understanding in relation to
politics today. They are so in a very simple, perhaps even a simplistic,
sense, a respect so crudely evident that it is not easy to imagine how
anyone could have the nerve to *deny* it, as opposed to letting their
thoughts pass it by discreetly on the other side. This superior honesty
of Plato's political and moral vision lies above all in its unflinching
recognition of the centrality of the combat between egoist impulses
and the dictates of rationality in recognizing the claims and needs and
sentiments of others within every single human being. We can
scarcely, even if we wished to, accept today Plato's view of the hierarchy of nature and reason or his over-readiness to ascribe substantive

66 Cf. David Hume, *A Treatise of Human Nature* (1739–40), Everyman ed. London 1911,
   Vol. 2, p. 127 (Bk II, Part 3, Section (1)): 'We speak not strictly and philosophically,
   when we talk of the combat of passion and of reason. Reason is, and ought only to be,
   the slave of the passions, and can never pretend to any other office than to serve and
   obey them.' And cf. the ringing affirmation (p. 128): 'It is not contrary to reason to
   prefer the destruction of the whole world to the scratching of my finger.'

egoism to animality and substantive altruism to abstract thought. We certainly face little temptation to share Plato's profound suspicion of the claims of the physical, of our bodies as such. We are inclined to see instead the grounds of hope for our species in the balance of natural animal affection against natural animal antipathy within its nature and to see the role of reason as no more crucial in extending the affection to increasingly wider categories of humans (and even non-human creatures) than it has so far, alas, proved in extending the antipathy. But even if we are right in making these assumptions, there are at least two respects in which Plato was profoundly right about the fundamentals of political theory in which most nineteenth century or twentieth century thinkers (especially, for example, Marx) were quite profoundly wrong. The first is that the moral queasiness of power, the perils and splendours of what can be caused to occur, within our collective social life, is something which not merely will never pass away from human history but simply never *could* – that the hope that by some automatic or even rationally chosen and intended mechanism human history could be purged of moral risk, could plug itself or find itself plugged as the destiny of complete societies or as a species in its entirety, into a grander historical variant of one of Robert Nozick's experience machines[67] and guaranteed that none but agreeable sensations could come its way, is as delusory to expect as it would be ignominious to choose. The second is that the vector of this collective destiny is the individual psyche, the field of choice, endlessly able to choose for the worse and endlessly able to strive for the better and necessarily and ceaselessly in consequence at war within itself.

Plato's explicitly political doctrine is certainly fairly grotesque, with its eminently sane assessment that power can only be trusted in the hands of the severely morally trustworthy and its eminently absurd allegation as to who precisely these severely trustworthy persons should be presumed to be. And even if his moral psychology was more comfortably plausible than we are apt to find it, so that the most knowing truly were the best and the most morally dependable, it is impossible for us to take seriously, even should we avoid succumbing to the most abject of relativisms, such a grossly restricted conception of

67 The theoretical purpose which Nozick intends his thought experiment to serve is to emphasize the priority of the human desire to act over the human desire to have acceptable experiences. (See Nozick, *Anarchy, State and Utopia*, pp. 42–5). It is not clear that such a conception of human nature is in any sense epistemically mandatory. But Nozick certainly makes it appear morally becoming: and if becoming at the individual level, then becoming also at the social level.

what the holders of power require to know. If only the best of human moral understanding could be adequate to direct human power morally, only the best of human practical causal understanding could be adequate to direct it practically. And the idea that these two twin skills could under any circumstances come to be seen as the monopoly of any distinct social group is evidently preposterous.

But if the best moral and practical insight of the species cannot be the prerogative of reliably distinguishable or specifiable groups of persons and if this realization dictates a hugely more democratic conception of political rights and capabilities than Plato favoured, it neither dictates nor indeed permits that ruthlessly evasive and disingenuous egalitarianism which pervades the ideologies of the modern world, capitalist and socialist alike, and pretends that the problems of power have been solved or would be solved if the power of men was rendered equal. And since the structural inequality of power in the societies of the modern world, however drastically reorganized these might be, is so intractably vast and since such power cannot be rendered safe, insulated from the capacity to harm, even in principle, it is clear enough that one of the most widely deplored characteristics of the Platonic Republic, the noble lie, has at least as guaranteed a place in any possible structures for our world as it had in that of Plato.

The noble lie[68] was the ideological basis of citizen compliance within the Republic. It was a lie in that what it propositionally asserted was contrary to fact. It was noble in that what it suggested was symbolically true. What it suggested amounted simply to the view that the philosopher rulers ought to hold power because they were wholly and uniquely fitted to do so and it suggested this (in Plato's eyes) practical enough truth in a form which was propositionally false because it was *ex hypothesi* beyond the imaginative capabilities of the majority of the population to grasp the full set of considerations which proved it to be true. This is not an agreeable line of thought. It underlines offensively the truth that in human social cooperation the disposition which

68 For the 'Noble lie' myth see Plato, *Republic*, 414 (Cornford (ed.) , *op. cit.*, pp. 103–4). Because the *Republic* is not in fact a blueprint for the practical design of a political community, the myth serves a less urgent purpose in Plato's exposition than, it is here insisted, its analogues must serve within the political life of a real society, however structurally admirable the latter may be. Cornford rejects the translation of the phrase as 'noble lie'. But since this is the form in which the phrase has become widely known, I have chosen to retain it. What is important in the present context is not the (false) suggestion that Plato was an enthusiastic advocate of manipulative propaganda but simply that he acknowledged the need for an ideological charter for the distribution of authority in his ideal society and that this charter was explicitly and necessarily mythical in character.

Bentham christened appropriate 'obsequiousness'[69] produces many practical advantages. But as yet at any rate there is no good reason to believe that we have devised a form of social organization in which the advantages which it produces will outweigh the disadvantages which flow from inappropriate obsequiousness. Claims at any time to have institutionalized authority are, then, necessarily false. But claims on the part of leaders to appropriate obsequiousness on particular occasions may perfectly well be valid.

Taken together, these two conclusions leave us with a discomfiting figure for the human cognitive political community in the face of its future: a most un-platonic Republic or set of republics facing a world of ambivalently promising and menacing human powers and unable in principle by any magical transformation to fix the promise and avert the menace in some permanent fashion, desperately in need of the best of its collective understanding, moral and practical, but unable to determine who precisely among its members possess this superior understanding, a world in which power is (and has to be) rendered psychically supportable (if at all) by the invention and rhetorical exposition of what are necessarily at best noble lies and lies of which it is hard in principle ever to know just how far they *are* noble. A species, the condition of which is broadly of this kind, is a species which can never be out of peril. But it is a species which can face its perils with very varying degrees of courage and sobriety and imagination.

What is hardest for us at present to discern with any confidence is how far our main failure thus far has been a failure of sobriety and how far it has been a failure of imagination. At present we certainly have no very satisfactory means for deciding how far it has always been a fantasy to hope to unite the intense moral fastidiousness of the western tradition with its equally intense commitment to the rational comprehension of reality – how far, that is to say, our moral sensibilities are in fact compatible with a recognition of real historical and natural possibilities. It is certainly an error to presume that there are no implicit contradictions between the values of the western tradition.[70] It is also,

69 For Bentham's emphasis on the indispensability of this orientation see James Steintrager, *Bentham*, pb. ed. London 1977, pp. 119–20.

70 Cf. for example, Goethe's comments on the antinomies between modern individualism and the importunities of political practice: 'The present condition of the world, with its demand for transparency in all relationships, is very favourable for the development of the individual, if he desires to keep himself to himself. But if he wishes to interfere with the running of the world's machinery, and thinks he can run some part of it according to his own independent ideas or check its working, then he will only come to grief all the more speedily' (quoted by Meinecke, *Historism*, p. 436).

at best, still an open question whether our sense of these values as objective and compelling is in any way epistemically justifed: whether these values are in fact, as we fondly suppose, anchored to any solid bed of external reality and not merely conferred on us by an essentially arbitrary caprice of our cultural history.[71]

In some respects our sobriety at present is distinctly defective: decadent or, as the eighteenth century would have termed it, corrupt. The expectation that we may yet contrive to unite in practice the full extent of our explicit moral concern for others with an enjoyment of our present entitlements to ease and comfort is less than plausible. If that is how we expect the future to be, we are exposing ourselves to most disagreeable surprises. 'For the dreamers of peace and happiness,' wrote Max Weber, 'there stands written over the door of mankind's unknown future "surrender all hope".'[72] Or, as Mao Tse-Tung more breezily put it: 'The life of sitting on sofas and using electric fans will not do.'[73] Advanced capitalist society cultivates in its citizens a mood which may very fairly be described as one of facile eudaemonism. To hope to extend such happiness as it makes available within itself to the vastly increased population of the world as a whole in the future without the most drastic political reorganization of this world and without considerable modification of the conception of happiness which it has fostered is not a coherent project. When St Just proclaimed to the Convention on 13th Ventose of the Year II that happiness was a new idea in Europe,[74] he no doubt exaggerated its novelty, just as

71 See e.g. John Adams, *Discourses from Davila* (1790), *The Works of John Adams*, ed. C. F. Adams, Vol. VI, Boston 1851, p. 281: 'Let us conclude with one reflection more which shall barely be hinted at, as delicacy, if not prudence, may require, in this place, some degree of reserve. Is there a possibility that the government of nations may fall into the hands of men who teach the most disconsolate of all creeds, that men are but fire-flies, and that this *all* is without a father? Is this the way to make man, as man, an object of respect? Or is to make murder itself as indifferent as shooting a plover, and the extermination of the Rohilla nation as innocent as the swallowing of mites on a morsel of cheese?' We must be as prudent as we can; but the time for delicacy is long past.

72 Inaugural Address at the University of Freiburg (1895), quoted here in David Beetham's translation from his *Max Weber and the Theory of Modern Politics*, p. 42.

73 Quoted from Frederic Wakeman Jr, *History and Will: Philosophical Perspectives of Mao Tse-Tung's Thought*, pb. ed. Berkeley, Calif. 1975, p. 305. (When he used this formula Mao was in fact addressing the Central Committee of the Party on the responsibilities of their station).

74 'Que l'Europe apprenne que vous ne voulez plus un malheureux ni un oppresseur sur le territoire française; que cet exemple fructifie sur la terre, qu'il y propage l'amour des vertus et le bonheur. Le bonheur est une idée neuve en Europe' (= 3 March 1794; Philippe Joseph Benjamin Buchez & Pierre C. Roux-Lavergne, *Historie Parlementaire de la révolution française*, Vol. XXXI, Paris 1837, p. 312).

when Adolf Hitler announced to the German people in the summer of 1933 that: 'The time of personal happiness is over',[75] he greatly overestimated the degree of its obsolescence. Indeed the expansion of capitalist production in the aftermath of the Second World War has since caused Hitler's prophecy (despite his own remarkable contribution to implementing it in practice) to seem simply absurd. But if the dream-time of capitalist society may fairly be conceived as a consciousness of entitlement to agreeable experiences without a morally rational conception of any schedule of duties attached to such entitlement, it is at least reasonable to assume that the dream will not last for ever.

There never has been and there never could have been a conception of capitalist society which both acknowledged in their entirety its factual properties in any instance and presented it as a morally rational order. Because it has always been morally vulnerable, it has also always been politically vulnerable, open to practical challenge, always from within and on occasion also – and now increasingly – from outside its own boundaries. For long it dealt with such challenges with remarkable success; and even now it shows in many settings an impressive capacity, politically and militarily, to fend for itself. It would certainly be silly to presume, as Marxists have recurrently hoped, that its political or military capacity to protect itself must suddenly and decisively falter. But it would be at least equally silly to presume that its proven capacity to protect itself in any particular setting in the past will guarantee its capacity to do so there in the future. If there were good reason to believe that capitalism was politically invulnerable, it might be a matter of little consequence that it has always been morally so vulnerable (so plainly premised ideologically on lies which lack any trace of nobility). If there were good reason to believe that it was politically doomed and fated to be replaced compulsively at some predestined pace by some other determinate form of society, irrespective of the moral properties of either, it would also, *ex hypothesi*, be a matter of small practical importance what these moral properties in fact were. In these circumstances we might have ample need for courage and sobriety but there would be little political call on our imaginations. But if the future which we face is not in this way guaranteed for better or for worse, there is great urgency for us to identify more clearly the range of real possibilities which it does offer. Most of the population of the world today does not inhabit advanced capitalist societies. Within

75 Quoted from Joachim C. Fest, *Hitler*, tr. R. & C. Winston, pb. ed. Harmondsworth 1977, p. 621.

advanced capitalist society, for the great majority of its citizens, there is certainly a great deal more than chains to lose. But for the inhabitants of both there may still be a world to win.

But then again, there may not. It is time that we devoted somewhat more of our collective imagination to reflecting seriously on whether there in fact is.

Index

Index